A NATURALIST'S GUIDE

BIRDS
OF
MYANMAR

Thet Zaw Naing, Robert Tizard & Geoffrey Davison

JOHN BEAUFOY PUBLISHING

First published in the United Kingdom in 2023 by John Beaufoy Publishing,
11 Blenheim Court, 316 Woodstock Road, Oxford OX2 7NS, England
www.johnbeaufoy.com

10 9 8 7 6 5 4 3 2 1

Photo credits

Front cover: *main image* Red Avadavat © Bikram Grewal; *bottom left* Thick-billed Pigeon © Chris Milligan; *bottom centre*
White-browed Nuthatch © Robert Tizard; *bottom right* Striped Laughingthrush © Thet Win.
Back cover: Gurney's Pitta © Thet Zaw Naing. **Title page:** Pheasant-tailed Jacana © Bikram Grewal. **Contents page:**
Stork-billed Kingfisher © Robert Tizard.

Main descriptions: photos are denoted by a page number followed by t (top), c (centre), b (bottom), l (left) or r (right).
James Eaton 23t, 79bl, 84br, 98b. **Bikram Grewal** 15bl, 18b, 22t, 22b, 27t, 34bl, 37b, 41t, 41br, 43bl, 44t, 45t, 45cr, 46t,
46b, 50t, 51bl, 53t, 54t, 54b, 55tr, 55bl, 56br, 59tl, 62b, 63t, 63br, 63bl, 67t, 79t, 80tl, 81b, 86tl, 86tr, 86b, 87t, 87b, 88t,
93b, 96tr, 96tl, 100b, 101tr, 103b, 104br, 107b, 109tl, 113b, 114tr, 114tl, 128b, 136t, 139bl, 140t, 142b, 143t, 143bl, 145b,
146br, 147t. **Nyan Lin** 18t, 24tl, 34br, 39b, 58br, 83t, 116tl, 122br, 122bl, 130t, 131t, 142t, 151tr. **Chris Milligan** 21t,
79br, 146bl. **Thet Zaw Naing** 12t, 14t, 14b, 15t, 16tl, 16b, 17t, 17bl, 19bl, 19br, 20t, 20b, 21b, 25t, 28t, 29t, 30t, 30b,
31bl, 32t, 34tr, 35t, 35b, 36tl, 38tl, 38br, 40tl, 40tr, 42b, 44cl, 44b, 45cl, 47bl, 47br, 48tl, 48tr, 48bl, 48br, 49tl, 49tr, 49b,
50bl, 50br, 51tr, 55tl, 55br, 56t, 56bl, 58t, 59tr, 60t, 61t, 61b, 64t, 65t, 65bl, 65br, 66t, 66b, 68tl, 68tr, 69t, 69b, 70t, 71t,
71b, 72t, 72b, 73t, 73b, 74t, 74b, 76t, 76b, 77t, 77br, 78bl, 78br, 79br, 80b, 81t, 82tl, 82tr, 82b, 83bl, 83br, 85t, 85bl, 85br,
86tc, 88b, 89tl, 89tr, 89bl, 89br, 90bl, 90br, 91t, 92tr, 92bl, 92br, 93t, 94t, 94bl, 94br, 95t, 95bl, 95br, 96bl, 96br, 97b,
98tl, 99t, 99bl, 99br, 103t, 104bc, 105t, 106b, 107tr, 108bl, 110b, 111t, 111b, 112t, 112b, 113t, 114b, 115t, 115b, 116tr,
117t, 119t, 120t, 120b, 121b, 122t, 123b, 125t, 125b, 126tl, 126tr, 126b, 127b, 129b, 133t, 133b, 134t, 135t, 135b, 136b,
137t, 137b, 138tl, 139t, 140b, 141t, 143br, 144br, 145t, 146t, 147b, 148br, 149b, 151bl, 151 br. **Robert Tizard** 12b, 15br,
16tr, 19t, 23b, 25t (need to add r and l with TZN) 26t, 26b, 27b, 28b, 29b, 31t, 31br, 32b, 33t, 33b, 34tl, 36tr, 36b, 37t,
38tr, 38bl, 39t, 40b, 41bl, 42t, 43br, 45bl, 45br, 47t, 51br, 52t, 52bl, 52br, 53b, 57t, 57bl, 57br, 58bl, 59b, 60b, 61t, 61c,
62t, 62c, 64b, 67b, 68b, 75t, 75b, 77bl, 78c, 80tr, 90t, 91b, 92tl, 95c, 97tr, 97tl, 98tr, 100t, 101tl, 101b, 102b, 104t, 104bl,
105b, 106t, 107tl, 108t, 108br, 109tr, 109b, 110t, 116b, 117b, 118tr, 118tl, 118b, 119b, 123t, 124t, 124b, 127tl, 127tr,
128t, 129tr, 130b, 131b, 132t, 132b, 134b, 138tr, 138tc, 139br, 141b, 144tl, 144tr, 144 bl, 148t, 148bl, 149t, 150t, 150b.
Wildlife Conservation Society 13t, 13b. **Lay Win** 17br, 24tr, 24b, 25b, 43t, 78t, 84t, 102t. **Thet Win** 84bl, 121t, 129tl,
138b, 151tl.

ISBN 978-1-909612-72-3

Edited by Krystyna Mayer
Designed by Alpana Khare Graphic Design
Project management by Rosemary Wilkinson

Printed and bound in Malaysia by Times Offset (M) Sdn. Bhd.

·Contents·

INTRODUCTION

Myanmar is at the centre of avian diversity in the Oriental region. Its location links the Himalaya to Sundaland, and the monsoon forests of Indochina to the very edge of the Indian plains. The country holds two areas of avian endemism with the xeric savannahs and shrub lands of the dry zone and the outlying ridges south of the Himalaya in the Chin Hills; it also includes the northernmost islands of the Andaman chain. This results in a very diverse avifauna of more than 1,150 species, including some of the best remaining populations of many of Asia's rarest birds.

The colonial past of Myanmar (formerly Burma) produced a relatively robust accounting of its avifauna before the country was closed off from the outside world. Its great ornithological history is reflected in the names of the birds themselves – Jerdon, Blyth, Hume and Davison, among others, all spent time in Myanmar or at least studying the country's birds.

Recent work by a growing number of Myanmar ornithologists and birders, along with outside collaborators and an increasing number of foreign birders, has begun to piece the full picture together. Using modern genetic techniques, we are also now unravelling the complexities of avian evolution; many new surprises will no doubt be revealed.

In developing the *Birds of Myanmar*, we chose a range of species, either those widespread in Myanmar or endemic or near-endemic species found in Myanmar's outstanding tourism destinations, such as the ancient temples of Bagan or the picturesque waters of Inle Lake. These special Myanmar species have been augmented with a selection of Asia's rarest and most threatened species that are still found in important populations in Myanmar such as Spoon-billed Sandpiper, White-bellied Heron and Gurney's Pitta.

CLIMATE

Myanmar has a monsoon climate with a pronounced hot season in March–May, followed by heavy rains over much of the country in late May–October, then a cool season in November–February. Despite the sometimes extreme weather, bird activity is high throughout the year.

ORNITHOLOGICAL REGIONS

The seven ornithological regions of Myanmar are based on Ben King's *Birds of Southeast Asia* 1975, then modified by Craig Robson in *A Field Guide to the Birds of Thailand and South-east Asia* 2008. The seven ornithological regions are: North, West, Central, East, South-west, South and Tenasserim. The modern name for Tenasserim is Tanintharyi (see map on inside front cover).

HABITATS & BIRD COMMUNITIES

Eastern Himalayas North Myanmar has an avifauna similar to Bhutan and Northeast India. It ranges from 200m to almost 6,000m and links tropical evergreen forests through temperate forests to snow fields on the slopes of Mt Hkakaborazi, the tallest mountain in Southeast Asia. These habitats hold classic Himalayan bird groups such as tragopans and other high-elevation pheasants, leaf warblers, ground babblers, laughingthrushes, thrushes and rosefinches.

Chin Hills West Myanmar has a similar avifauna to the north, but many birds have evolved into unique species found only here and in neighbouring Northeast India. The hills reach to over 3,000m and support the endemic White-browed Nuthatch, as well as near-endemic races of flycatchers, laughingthrushes and sunbirds, in the warm temperate rainforest with oaks and rhododendrons above 2,000m.

Dry Zone Central Myanmar is surrounded by ridges separating the floodplain of the Ayeyarwady River from Rakhine State to the west and Shan State to the east. This unique area of heavily populated and cultivated savannahs and dry forests has a number of endemic birds, including the White-throated Babbler, Hooded Treepie and Jerdon's Minivet. These are easily found around the World Heritage temples of Bagan and the gardens of Naypyidaw.

Shan Plateau East Myanmar is an extensive plateau crossing the Thanlwin (Salween) River to the Mekong. Here, rolling hills of oak and pine forests hold many species familiar from Thailand and Indochina. On the western side of the plateau, Inle Lake links the forests in the hills with bird-rich wetlands, and attractive and welcoming communities around the lake.

Arakan South-west Myanmar is a forested ridge separating the Ayeyarwady floodplain to the coast of the Bay of Bengal. These forests are linked to the ecology of Bangladesh and are still rarely visited and poorly understood. Off the south-west corner of Myanmar there are a few scattered islands linking Myanmar to the Andaman Islands in India. These coral-encircled islands have not been surveyed since colonial times and hold yet more of Myanmar's evolutionary trophies still to be explored.

Ayeyarwady Delta South Myanmar is an extensive area of rice fields and wetlands stretching from Yangon to where the Ayeyarwady meets the sea. This area still holds one of the world's greatest remaining populations of Sarus Cranes, and a range of shy grassland residents and large flocks of wintering migrant birds visiting from the eastern Palearctic.

Tenasserim Peninsula Tenasserim is the long, thin border between the 800 plus islands of the Mergui Archipelago to the eastern border with Thailand. The remaining tropical evergreen forests here link to the northernmost end of the Kra Peninsula and the birds of Sundaland. They include the last remaining Gurney's Pittas on the planet, as well as some of the few remaining populations of Sundaic species in Myanmar.

BIRD IDENTIFICATION

Many aspects should be taken into consideration when attempting to identify an unfamiliar species. Size, shape, colours, patterns, call, behaviour, habitat and location can all help an observation. Even taking note of the way birds walk or move in flight could be the clincher. The illustrations on page 10 show the most common ways to refer to certain parts of a bird to describe its physical appearance. Some species look very similar, especially groups such as pipits and leaf warblers, so always consider several options. A decent record photograph is useful for identification purposes, enabling you to share your sightings with others and receive a second opinion.

MIGRATION

Myanmar sits along two major flyways: the Central Asian Flyway linking the country to central Russia, Central Asia and the Tibetan Plateau, and the East Asian-Australasian Flyway linking it to the Korean Peninsula, Japan, eastern China and Russia. Bird migration in Myanmar has been relatively little studied and there is still much to learn. The discovery of globally important populations of wintering Spoon-billed Sandpipers only occurred within the past decade.

BIRD CONSERVATION

There are 1,153 bird species recorded in Myanmar, 15 per cent of which are globally threatened or near threatened. This includes 12 Critically Endangered species, 17 Endangered species, 43 Vulnerable species and 99 Near Threatened species. Several Endangered species are possibly Extinct in Myanmar, including the Pink-headed Duck, White-shouldered Ibis and Greater Adjutant. Nonetheless, Myanmar continues to support some of the most globally important populations of Critically Endangered birds in the world, including Baer's Pochard, White-bellied Heron, Spoon-billed Sandpiper, White-rumped, Red-headed and Slender-billed Vultures, Helmeted Hornbill, Gurney's Pitta and Yellow-breasted Bunting.

These species are facing a range of threats, including habitat loss through the destruction and fragmentation of habitat, loss of forests, plains and other natural systems to industrial agriculture, mining and urban developments, including the draining of swamps and other wetlands, which reduce potential habitat for many species. Wetland species are further threatened by liberal pesticide use across much of the agricultural landscape.

Hunting, snaring, poisoning and egg collecting have reduced populations of large frugivores such as hornbills in some areas, as well as game birds such as waterfowl, pheasants and partridges. Some of these species are sold into local and international markets. This trade includes local consumption as bush meat, small passerines caught for merit release at local temples, pet trade for parakeets and mynas, and even commercial hunting of hornbills, especially the Helmeted Hornbill for its casques, to be carved into trinkets for sale in China.

Bird conservation is important because birds are sensitive to habitat change and are easy to see and record. They are an important tool for ecologists to measure the health of environments, and whether ecosystems are managed for wild lands, agricultural production, water or tourism, successes can be measured by the health and diversity of bird populations.

Fortunately, bird species are being actively conserved in Myanmar, through a number of important conservation organizations and the government. As the loss and destruction of habitat is the most serious threat facing many birds in Myanmar, government and conservation organizations tasked with protecting birds work to develop and manage protected areas, as well as conducting research, education and outreach. The Ministry of Natural Resources and Environmental Conservation, in particular the Forest Department and Nature and Environmental Conservation Division, have been responsible for wildlife protection since the Burma Forest Act of 1902 and the new Conservation of Biodiversity and Protected Areas Law 2018. The law highlights habitat maintenance and restoration, and protection of endangered and protected bird species.

The government currently recognizes 45 protected areas, covering about 6.1 per cent (25,573km^2) of the total area of Myanmar. They stretch from the snowy mountain peaks in the far north, to Lampi island in the far south, and include some of the largest intact forest blocks remaining in Southeast Asia.

Myanmar is party to several regional and international agreements, such as migratory waterbird conservation for the East Asian-Australasian Flyway Partnership (EAAFP), and the Convention on the Conservation of Migratory Species (CMS), which aim to conserve migratory bird species within their migratory ranges. Local and international organizations (p. 172) work in close partnership with the government and neighbouring countries to develop single-species action plans to protect globally threatened birds such as the White-bellied Heron, vultures, Gurney's Pitta and Spoon-billed Sandpiper.

Birdwatching in Myanmar

Despite Myanmar's relative isolation, regular birdwatching tours have been coming to the country since the mid-1990s. They are supported by a reasonable number of skilled local guides who are visiting key sites and finding new areas to explore on a regular basis.

Yangon Most international visitors enter Myanmar through the international airport at Yangon. The city is developing quickly but still holds a few areas worthy of exploration. There are a number of city parks that hold a good variety of birds, in particular the area around Shwedagon Pagoda, which has a variety of resident species and can turn up surprises during migration. The area often hosts a massive roost of Wrinkle-lipped Bats during the colder months of the year (November–February), and their emergence each evening at around 6.00 p.m. attracts good numbers of raptors looking for an easy meal. These include the Peregrine Falcon, Eurasian Kestrel, Black Kite, Shikra and Eurasian

Sparrowhawk. On the northern edge of the city is Hlawga Park, which holds a mix of forest, scrub and wetland habitats. The park hosts a large roost of more than 1,000 Asian Openbills. On occasion the rare and unpredictable Pale-capped Pigeon occurs here, and it is the best site to search for the endemic Pale-eyed Bulbul. Heading further north past the city of Bago, Moeyungyi Wetland, Myanmar's first Ramsar Site, provides a great weekend getaway from the city to see a range of waterbirds. There is a guesthouse on the lakeside and boats and guides can be hired locally.

Bagan Easily Myanmar's greatest cultural attraction, the thousands of ancient temples here also provide a magnificent backdrop to search for the country's main endemic species. The White-throated Babbler, Burmese Bushlark, Hooded Treepie, Jerdon's Minivet, Burmese Prinia, Ayeyarwady Bulbul and Burmese Collared Dove are all found within walking distance of the main temples. Laggar Falcons, Spotted Owlets and Plain-backed Sparrows nest directly on the temples. The river at Bagan yields even more avian treasures, with a great variety of waterbirds and some restricted range species on the grassy islands in the river. These include the White-tailed Stonechat, Sand Lark, Striated Babbler and, occasionally, Red Avadavat.

Natmataung National Park From Bagan you can drive west into the Chin Hills and Natmataung National Park. The road passes through a fascinating transition of habitats, leaving the dry zone behind and passing through extensive dry deciduous forests before entering evergreen montane forests and eventually the oak and rhododendron community that is home to Myanmar's rarest endemic, the White-browed Nuthatch. The park holds a number of other endemics, including the Burmese Tit and Mount Victoria Babax, as well as some restricted range babblers including the Spot-breasted Scimitar-babbler, Striped and Brown-capped Laughingthrushes and – although it is seldom seen – the near mythical Blyth's Tragopan.

Inle Lake Beautiful Inle Lake hosts some incredible birding opportunities, and a boat trip on the northern end of the lake provides an opportunity to search for the enigmatic Jerdon's Bushchat, Chinese Grassbird and a variety of breeding and wintering waterbirds, occasionally including the Critically Endangered Baer's Pochard. Heading uphill from the lake into the Shan Yoma leads to the colonial hill station of Kalaw. This area provides a welcome respite from the heat of the plains, and a completely different set of montane species when compared to Natamataung National Park. Search here for the Black-backed Sibia, Spectacled Barwing, Black-headed Greenfinch and restricted range Burmese Yuhina, which is endemic to this range of mountains that barely sneak into a small corner of northern Thailand.

Increasingly interesting for resident birders is the variety of wetland areas around Mandalay. Places such as Paleik In and Phyu In have turned up a number of vagrants for Myanmar, including Bean and White-fronted Geese. They are also good areas to search for shy, retiring rail species such as the White-browed Crake and Eastern Water

Rail. Extensive searching may even turn up a few wintering Baer's Pochards, a Critically Endangered species that still winters in small numbers in central Myanmar.

As peace has been returning to the remotest corners of Myanmar, opportunities for exploration further off the beaten path have been expanding. Some areas will soon become more accessible, including Southern Taninthayi, the home of the world's last Gurney's Pittas and the fascinating northern tip of Sundaland. Many species are only found in this region, making it unique for the country. A variety of hornbills, pigeons, woodpeckers and night birds awaits the adventurous birder. Closer to Yangon but still quite difficult to access, the amazing coastal resources of the Gulf of Mottama and Northern Rakhine coast hold some of the largest wintering numbers of Spoon-billed Sandpipers, along with hundreds of thousands of wintering waders, terns and gulls. Most of these areas can only be accessed by boat, but this is increasingly possible with the support of local tour groups in Yangon.

The other great unexplored territory in Myanmar is the far north. Vast areas of forest still stretch along the border with India, Tibet and Yunnan, holding a fascinating array of eastern Himalayan species. Tragopans, monals, Ward's Trogons, Beautiful Nuthatches, White-bellied Herons, Fire-tailed Myzornis and an incredible array of laughingthrushes and babblers can be found in these areas. While access is still challenging, many of these birds can be found on trekking trips into the far corners of Kachin State and Sagaing Region – again, these need the support of local tour groups that are increasingly offering trips to this region.

CLASSIFICATION

The classification or taxonomy of birds from Myanmar has followed Robson (2008) for many years, but it is now going through a number of changes with several distinctive forms recently or soon to be elevated to species. This book follows the *Handbook of Birds of the World* and the *Birdlife Taxonomic Checklist* for the order of species, supplemented by the most recent taxonomic information, some still in preparation for publication, for the classification of endemic species. Increased research on the morphology, distribution and genetics of Myanmar's birds is likely to produce additional species-level splits.

DOCUMENTING YOUR BIRD RECORDS

There are a growing number of technical systems to help collect, identify and review the birds you have recorded, and share them with a broader community of scientists, researchers, naturalists and wildlife enthusiasts. These include eBird, iGoTerra and iNaturalist.

BIRD TOPOGRAPHY

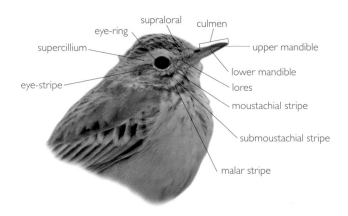

supraloral

culmen

eye-ring

supercillium

upper mandible

eye-stripe

lower mandible

lores

moustachial stripe

submoustachial stripe

malar stripe

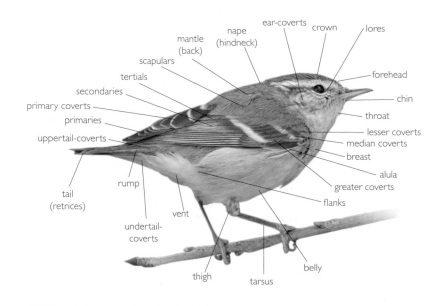

ear-coverts

crown

lores

nape
(hindneck)

mantle
(back)

scapulars

forehead

tertials

secondaries

chin

primary coverts

throat

primaries

lesser coverts

uppertail-coverts

median coverts

breast

alula

tail
(retrices)

rump

greater coverts

flanks

vent

undertail-
coverts

belly

thigh

tarsus

aberrant Abnormal or unusual.

adult Mature; capable of breeding.

aerial Making use of the open sky.

aquatic Living on or in water.

arboreal Living in trees.

canopy Leafy foliage of treetops.

casque Growth above bill of hornbills.

cheek Term loosely applied to sides of head, below eye or on ear-coverts.

collar Distinctive band of colour encircling or partly encircling neck.

coverts Small feathers on wings, ear and base of tail.

crepuscular Active at dusk and dawn.

crest Extended feathers on head.

crown-stripe Distinct line from forehead along centre of crown.

ear-coverts Feathers covering ear opening; often distinctly coloured.

endemic Indigenous and confined to a place

extinct No longer in existence.

eye-ring Contrasting ring around eye.

family Specified group of genera.

flank Side of body.

foraging Searching for food.

foreneck Lower throat.

form Subspecies.

gape Basal part of beak.

genus Group of related species.

hackles Long and pointed neck feathers.

hepatic Rust- or liver-coloured plumage phase, mainly in female cuckoos.

iris Coloured eye membrane surrounding pupil.

Isthmus of Kra The narrowest part of the Malay Peninsula.

lanceolate Lance shaped; slim and pointed.

malar stripe Stripe on side of throat.

mandible Each of the two parts of bill.

mantle Back, between wings.

mask Dark plumage around eyes and ear coverts.

morph One of several distinct types of plumage in the same species.

moult Seasonal shedding of plumage.

nocturnal Active at night.

nominate subspecies First subspecies to be formally named.

non-passerine All orders of birds except for passerines.

order Group of related families.

paleartic Old World and Arctic zone.

pelagic Ocean-going.

pied Black and white.

plumage Feathers of a bird.

primaries Outer flight feathers in wing.

race Subspecies.

range Geographical area or areas inhabited by a species.

raptors Birds of prey and vultures, excluding owls.

rump Lower back.

scapulars Feathers along edge of mantle.

secondaries Inner wing feathers.

spangles Distinctive white or shimmering spots in plumage.

speculum Area of colour on secondary feathers of wings.

species Groups of birds (or other animals and plants) reproductively isolated from other such groups.

storey Level of a tree or forest.

streamers Long extensions to feathers, usually of tail.

subspecies Distinct form that does not have specific status.

Sundaland (also called the Sundaic region) This is a biogeographical region of Southeast Asia from southernmost Myanmar to Malaysia and Indonesia.

supercilium Eyebrow, stripe above eye.

supraloral Area above lore.

talons Strong, sharp claws used to seize or kill prey.

tarsus Lower part of a bird's legs.

terminal band Broad band on tip of feather or tail.

tertials Innermost wing-coverts, often covering secondaries.

underparts Undersurface of a bird from throat to vent.

underwing Undersurface of a wing including linings and flight feathers.

upperparts Upper surface of a bird including wings, back and tail.

vagrant Accidental, irregular.

vent Undertail area.

wing-coverts Small feathers on wing at bases of primaries and secondaries.

wingspan Length from one wing-tip to the other when fully extended.

winter plumage Plumage seen during non breeding winter months.

yoma Low mountains or hills.

Green Peafowl ■ *Pavo muticus* 180–250cm

DESCRIPTION Huge, magnificent pheasant with iridescent green plumage. Male has impressively large train – this is fanned out above the back to impress the more modestly

plumed female. When seen well, reveals intricate head pattern of yellow and pale blue skin surrounded by iridescent green feathers, including several long plumes sticking straight up from top of head. **DISTRIBUTION** Formerly across Myanmar but now restricted to a few protected areas and community areas in North, Central and East where it is not hunted. **HABITAT AND HABITS** Often found along forested streams and rivers, but also occurs in open deciduous and pine forests, wandering into agricultural fields to feed. **STATUS** Uncommon and declining, due to hunting.

Red Junglefowl ■ *Gallus gallus* 65–78cm

DESCRIPTION Wild ancestor of domestic chicken. Male displays impressive red head, golden neck, maroon back, black belly, black and gold wings, and sickle-shaped green

tail, often with thin white tuft of feathers on rump. Female subdued browns with golden cast on neck and fine dark vermiculations on each feather. **DISTRIBUTION** Throughout Myanmar. **HABITAT AND HABITS** Found from lowlands into middle hills, often in areas of bamboo or feeding on riverbanks with forested edges. Often occurs in pairs or small groups; sometimes several females with single male. May follow groups of elephants or wild pigs. **STATUS** Common resident. In certain areas reduced by hunting and snaring.

Blyth's Tragopan ■ *Tragopan blythii* 65–70cm

DESCRIPTION Stunning male has yellow face, deep orange head and neck, brown back, wings finely patterned with black vermiculation and small, star-like white spots, and pale grey belly. Female warm chocolate-brown overall with similar black vermiculation and white spots. **DISTRIBUTION** At 1,500–2,600m in higher mountains in West and North Myanmar. Occasionally seen in Natmataung National Park and mountains of far north. **HABITAT AND HABITS** Found in mixed oak and rhododendrons, and adjoining areas of montane evergreen forest. Very shy and difficult to see due to retiring habits and heavy hunting pressure across range. **STATUS** Rare resident. Threatened by hunting.

Kalij Pheasant ■ *Lophura leucomelanos* 63–74cm

DESCRIPTION Highly variable species with several races across Myanmar. All have red faces. Male has black crest. Southeastern birds grey with intricate black and white streaking on back, neck and wings extending on to tail. Birds get increasingly darker in West, with reduced white streaking, eventually becoming all black with white rump in northwestern race. Female shows less variability; variations on brown and white patterns similar to male. **DISTRIBUTION** Mainly Tenasserim, West and North Myanmar. **HABITAT AND HABITS** Occurs in evergreen forests in lowlands to middle hills. Primarily in forest and rarely out in the open; usually seen running across roads. **STATUS** Uncommon resident. Reduced by hunting and snaring in certain areas.

Lesser Whistling-duck ■ *Dendrocygna javanica* 38–42cm

DESCRIPTION Large brown duck with dark bill, dark cap, chestnut wing-coverts and white undertail. **DISTRIBUTION** Throughout Myanmar. Regularly heard over urban centres such as Yangon and Naypyidaw at night. **HABITAT AND HABITS** Resident of

wetlands, often forming large flocks. At night regularly disperses more widely to feed in rice fields and other wetland areas. Flocks easily heard as they utter twittering whistle while flying overhead. **STATUS** Common resident throughout, but numbers reduced by hunting and poisoning in some areas; sold locally for food.

Bar-headed Goose ■ *Anser indicus* 71–76cm

DESCRIPTION Large white and grey goose with two distinctive dark bars on head, black and white neck, and bright yellow bill and legs. **DISTRIBUTION** West, Central and North Myanmar. **HABITAT AND HABITS** Found on large rivers and wetlands, often in flocks of tens to hundreds, occasionally with other geese and ducks. Famed as a high-altitude migrant over Himalaya. **STATUS** Uncommon. Numbers reduced by hunting and poisoning in some areas; sold locally for food.

Greylag Goose ■ *Anser anser* 76–89cm

DESCRIPTION Wild ancestor of domestic goose. Large, warm grey goose with pink bill and legs. **DISTRIBUTION** Central and North Myanmar. **HABITAT AND HABITS** Found on large rivers and wetlands, often in flocks of tens to hundreds, occasionally with other geese and ducks. **STATUS** Common but local winter visitor. Numbers reduced by hunting and poisoning in some areas; sold locally for food.

Goosander ■ *Mergus merganser* 60–72cm

DESCRIPTION Striking white and black long, slender duck. Male has iridescent green head. Female has chestnut head with white chin and throat, and long, serrated red bill. **DISTRIBUTION** North Myanmar, where there are fast-flowing, clear streams. **HABITAT AND HABITS** Found along fast-flowing rivers, especially in clear water, often forming large groups. Hunts for fish by diving and pursuing them underwater. **STATUS** Common winter visitor to North. Numbers reduced by hunting.

Ruddy Shelduck ▪ *Tadorna ferruginea* 61–70cm

DESCRIPTION Large orange duck with pale head; white and black and iridescent green in wings. In Burmese language referred to as 'Hintha', a reference to the waterfowl with golden neck feathers seen by two princes who founded Bago Kingdom. **DISTRIBUTION** Along Ayeyarwady and Chindwin Rivers and their tributaries; less common along Mekong. Also wetland areas in North and Central Myanmar. **HABITAT AND HABITS** Found in large rivers and wetlands. Occurs in pairs but often forms large flocks before roosting for the night. **STATUS** Common winter visitor from breeding areas on Tibetan Plateau. Numbers reduced by hunting and poisoning in some areas; sold locally for food.

Cotton Pygmy-goose ▪ *Nettapus coromandelianus* 30–38cm

DESCRIPTION Small white and green goose with clean white cheeks and black crown; bright green wings with white band. Female duller than male with dark crown and eye-stripe; in flight shows much less white in wings. **DISTRIBUTION** Throughout Myanmar. Regular in wetlands in and around Yangon, Naypyidaw and Mandalay. **HABITAT AND HABITS** Found in wetlands and flooded fields; occasionally in rice fields but rarely on rivers. Quite retiring, often sticking close to areas of floating vegetation. Often in pairs and occasionally forms large flocks. **STATUS** Common resident.

White-winged Duck
■ *Asarcornis scutulata* 66–81cm

DESCRIPTION Large dark duck with white head and finely speckled black neck. In flight shows large white wing-patch and smaller patch of pale blue feathers on secondaries. **DISTRIBUTION** Remaining population found in North; formerly found in forested areas throughout Myanmar. **HABITAT AND HABITS** Restricted to forest pools and streams, occasional dispersing into more open wetlands and rice fields at night, usually singly or in pairs. **STATUS** Rare resident. Globally endangered due to habitat loss, disturbance and hunting.

Ferruginous Pochard ■ *Aythya nyroca* 38–42cm;
Baer's Pochard ■ *A. baeri* 41–47cm

DESCRIPTION Warm chestnut-brown ducks with prominent white eye. In flight show predominantly white flight feathers. Female duller that male, with dark eye. Much rarer Baer's darker than Ferruginous, with male revealing blackish-green sheen to head, brown breast and strongly demarcated pale sides when at rest. Females very similar but with dark eye and paler sides. **DISTRIBUTION** North, East and occasionally Central Myanmar. **HABITAT AND HABITS** Wetlands and large rivers, and occasionally forested streams. Usually in pairs or small groups, occasionally mixed with other species. Feed by diving regularly. Found in deepest parts of wetland. **STATUS** Uncommon winter visitor (Ferruginous); winter visitor (Baer's). Baer's known to hybridize with Ferruginous due to very few remaining mates of its own species.

Ferruginous Pochard *Baer's Pochard*

Indian Spot-billed Duck ■ *Anas poecilorhyncha* 58–63cm

DESCRIPTION Large, mottled grey and brown duck with big white wing-patch. Dark bill

with yellow tip, dark crown and line through eye when seen well. **DISTRIBUTION** Throughout Myanmar. Most common in Central and North. **HABITAT AND HABITS** Often found on wetlands and rivers. Can form large flocks in some areas, often mixed with other waterfowl. **STATUS** Common resident. However, numbers reduced by hunting and poisoning in some areas, and sold locally for food.

Little Grebe ■ *Tachybaptus ruficollis* 25–29cm

DESCRIPTION Small, duck-like bird. When breeding has yellow eyes, chestnut face and throat, and dark crown, neck and body. Shows paler sides when at rest, and often shows pale tuft of tail. In non-breeding plumage much paler buff on head, neck and sides. Rarely seen to fly but often skitters across the water as if trying to take off when alarmed. **DISTRIBUTION** Throughout lowlands. **HABITAT AND HABITS** Found on wetlands, small pools and occasionally rivers. Feeds by diving and often hides at edges of reeds or grass. Rarely flies and often sinks out of site when approached too closely. **STATUS** Common resident.

Burmese Collared-dove ▪ *Streptopelia xanthocycla* 30–32cm ⓔ

DESCRIPTION Light pinkish-brown dove with yellow eye-ring; very pale tone on head, neck and breast, deeper on back and wings. White-bordered black patch on neck-sides. Juveniles sandier brown than adults, at first having only trace of neck-patch. In flight, shows large white corners to square tail, and dark primaries contrast with pale grey carpals and secondaries. Previously regarded as race of the **Eurasian Collared-dove** *S. decaocto*. **DISTRIBUTION** Endemic to Central Myanmar. **HABITAT AND HABITS** Found in dry open woodland, scrub and farmland in lowlands. Calls with low, soft *coo-cooo-cu* from tree perch, and nests in trees. **STATUS** Uncommon local resident. Numbers reduced by hunting and sold locally for food.

Red Turtle-dove ▪ *Streptopelia tranquebarica* 20–23cm;
Oriental Turtle-dove ▪ *S. orientalis* 33–35cm

DESCRIPTION Small, short-tailed doves. Male rich rosy-brown with grey head and rump. Female similar but paler sandy-brown. Both sexes of adults (but not juveniles) have black hindneck-ring. Oriental much larger than Red, with dark scalloping on brown back and wings, and several black bars forming patch on neck. **DISTRIBUTION** Throughout Myanmar. **HABITAT AND HABITS** Red found in dry, open country with scattered trees and rural landscapes to about 1,200m; Oriental in similar or more forested habitat to 2,300m. **STATUS** Common resident (Red); locally common resident and occasional winter migrant (Oriental).

Red Turtle-dove

Oriental Turtle-dove

Eastern Spotted Dove ■ *Spilopelia chinensis* 27–30cm

DESCRIPTION Overall light brown, with slight pinkish hue, and plumage with darker upperparts; black patch with white spots across nape diagnostic; white vent; light yellow

iris; red feet. **DISTRIBUTION** Widespread from Bangladesh to southern China, Taiwan to the Philippines. Throughout most of Myanmar. **HABITAT AND HABITS** Inhabits open country, scrub, plantations, gardens and villages. Usually seen singly or in pairs, feeding on the ground or engaged in courtship. Takes off when disturbed at close quarters. **STATUS** Common resident, though often kept as cage bird.

Asian Emerald Dove ■ *Chalcophaps indica* 23–27cm

DESCRIPTION Handsome dove with diagnostic emerald-green wings with black primaries. Crown greyish and underparts dull maroon. Bill red, legs greyish-pink. Male brighter than female, with whiter brow and three bold dark and light grey bands across back and rump. **DISTRIBUTION** Forested areas across Myanmar, North, West, South-

west, East, South and Tenasserim. **HABITAT AND HABITS** Keeps to the ground in forests, forest edges, mangroves and plantations. Usually solitary, feeding on fallen seeds and grubs. Flight generally low between trees, with rapid wingbeats. Call a soft, low *tick-Whooo*, repeated monotonously. Calling birds may remain at a site for several weeks before moving on. **STATUS** Uncommon resident.

Thick-billed Green-pigeon

■ *Treron curvirostra* 24–31cm

DESCRIPTION In both sexes, overall plumage olive-green, with yellow wing-bars, light green eye-ring, thick bill with maroon at base, and red legs. Adult male has maroon mantle and wing-coverts; vent cinnamon. Female has darker olive-green wing-coverts. **DISTRIBUTION** Throughout Myanmar. **HABITAT AND HABITS** Frequents mangroves, well-wooded gardens, forest edges and forests. Usually seen in canopy or middle storey. Often feeds in large flocks (sometimes 50 birds simultaneously) in fruiting fig trees, at times with other frugivorous birds. **STATUS** Locally common. Numbers reduced by hunting and sold locally for food.

Yellow-footed Green-pigeon ■ *Treron phoenicopterus* 33cm

DESCRIPTION Bright green and yellow with grey head and belly, and intervening bright yellow neck, collar and breast. Tail yellow-green at base and grey at tip. **DISTRIBUTION** Resident from Pakistan to southern China. Throughout Myanmar at lower elevations. **HABITAT AND HABITS** Found in semi-deciduous forests and secondary growth to above 1,200m, calling with long series of deep whistles flowing up and down the scale. Occurs in large flocks concentrated in fruiting trees. **STATUS** Locally common. Numbers reduced by hunting and sold locally for food.

Green Imperial-pigeon ■ *Ducula aenea* 40–47cm

DESCRIPTION Heavy, bulky pigeon with pale grey head, neck and underparts, and deep bronze-green wings, back and tail. In flight, broad, square tail and chestnut

undertail-coverts are seen. DISTRIBUTION Indian subcontinent to southern China south to the Philippines, Indonesia and Sulawesi. In Myanmar widespread but rather local. HABITAT AND HABITS Found in crowns of tall forest trees, in lowlands below 900m, flying long distances over canopy. When settled, gives deep, booming calls, *wu-whruuu*. STATUS Uncommon and declining, with healthy populations mostly restricted to lowland forests inside protected areas.

Mountain Imperial-pigeon ■ *Ducula badia* 43–51cm

DESCRIPTION Big, sombre pigeon with light grey plumage and whitish or light grey

throat; mantle, wings and tail dark brown or cinnamon; legs pink. DISTRIBUTION Throughout Myanmar, mostly above 400m. HABITAT AND HABITS One of the common pigeons seen in montane forests. Remains in tree crowns and can be inconspicuous until it moves or calls. One or two often seen feeding together with other frugivores at fruiting fig trees. Call a deep, resonating *whoo-Whoomp*. STATUS Common resident in mountains and hills.

Hodgson's Frogmouth
■ *Batrachostomus hodgsoni* 22–27cm

DESCRIPTION Hard to identify but one of only two frogmouth species in Myanmar. Male heavily vermiculated all over, including grey (not rufous) breast lacking any clear white spots. Female plain bright rufous, with white collar complete in front and behind, and second band of white spots across lower breast. **DISTRIBUTION** Northeast India to Southwest China. West, North and East Myanmar. **HABITAT AND HABITS** Found in evergreen broadleaved and coniferous forests in hills, usually at 900–1,900m. Nocturnal, giving up to 10 rising, slightly tremulous whistles, at intervals of a few seconds. **STATUS** Uncommon resident.

Indian Nightjar ■ *Caprimulgus asiaticus* 23–24cm

DESCRIPTION Small, rather short-tailed, pale nightjar with buff collar and wide buff margins to scapulars, and two white throat-patches; small white patch on primaries and white outer corners to tail seen in flight. **DISTRIBUTION** India to Thailand and Indochina. Throughout Myanmar in suitable dry habitats, except North. Regularly found around temples in Bagan. **HABITAT AND HABITS** Nocturnal, in dry open forest and scrub, in lowlands and foothills. Male's call a short series of knocking or clucking sounds, the first few slow and the rest speeding up and fading. **STATUS** Uncommon resident.

Whiskered Treeswift ▪ *Hemiprocne comata* 15–17cm;
Crested Treeswift ▪ *H. coronata* 23–25cm

DESCRIPTION Treeswifts are slim, erect birds with long wings (tips crossed when perched) and deeply forked tail. Whiskered small, slim and brown, with two white lines on sides of head (brow and moustache), and white on innermost wing feathers. Ear-coverts between two white lines maroon in male, blackish in female. Much more common Crested substantially bigger, ashy-grey with dark wings; male has rufous face and throat.
DISTRIBUTION Whiskered only in southern Tenasserim. Crested throughout Myanmar.

Whiskered Treeswift   *Crested Treeswift*

HABITAT AND HABITS Often seen perched on end twigs of tree crowns, or in flight over lowland and hill forests. Makes short flights after insects, typically returning to the same perch. Nest a tiny white cup adhering to exposed tree-top bough, built by both sexes, which alternate in bringing nest material and in incubation. **STATUS** Locally common.

Germain's Swiftlet ▪ *Aerodramus germani* 11.5–12.5cm

DESCRIPTION Field identification of swiftlets notoriously difficult. Germain's small with

moderate tail-notch and somewhat pale rump; otherwise resembles other swiftlet species in being all dark above and below. In breeding colonies, whitish (rather than blackish or moss-laden) nest a good guide. **DISTRIBUTION** Southeast Asia (Malaysia and Indonesia). In Myanmar originally known from Tenasserim but now commercially raised along coast to Yangon. **HABITAT AND HABITS** Flies rapidly over forest canopy, agricultural land and gardens, and in towns. Nests in dark spaces like caves, and increasingly in abandoned buildings and modified concrete structures. Clean white nests raised commercially for birdnest soup and other products that provide significant profits for local people. **STATUS** Uncommon. Coastal and expanding in Myanmar.

Asian Palm-swift ■ *Cypsiurus balasiensis* 11–13cm
Pacific Swift ■ *Apus pacificus* 17–19.5cm

DESCRIPTION Slim, with narrow, pointed wings; dark grey-brown above and slightly paler below and on rump. Tail rather long, slender, and often held compactly as single point but revealed as deeply forked when bird steers. Good identification point is sweeping, upwards flight to land within leafy crowns of tree palms. Asian Palm-swift can be confused with several larger Apus swifts including Pacific, **Blyth's Swift** *Apus leuconyx*, **Cook's Swift** *Apus cooki* and **Dark-rumped Swift** *Apus acuticauda*. **DISTRIBUTION** South and Southeast Asia ranging to Indonesia and the Philippines. Common throughout Myanmar where fan-leafed palms are available. **HABITAT AND HABITS** Seen over tree plantations, orchards, gardens, parks and villages, where there are tall, fan-leafed palms available for nesting. Nest a fluffy white pad adhering to undersurface of hanging leaf, or alternatively within palm-thatched roofs of village houses. Rapid, direct flight interrupted by skittering changes of direction. **STATUS** Common.

Pacific Swift   Asian Palm-swift

House Swift ■ *Apus nipalensis* 14–15cm

DESCRIPTION Medium-sized dark swift, bigger than swiftlets, with glossy black plumage and prominent white rump; throat white; tail slightly notched. **DISTRIBUTION** Along Himalaya, through Southeast Asia, to Indonesia and the Philippines, and ranging north into southern China and Japan. In Myanmar common in towns and often breeds in pagodas, as at Shwedagon. **HABITAT AND HABITS** Prefers open country, forest edges, towns and cities. Often forms large breeding colonies under eaves of man-made structures such as buildings or bridges, cliffs or cave mouths. Gregarious in nature. Can be very noisy at dusk when returning to roost. **STATUS** Common.

Greater Coucal ▪ *Centropus sinensis* 47–52cm

DESCRIPTION Large, crow-like bird with heavy, clumsy flight and long, floppy tail. Overall plumage glossy black; wings chestnut and eyes red. **DISTRIBUTION** Widespread

in South and Southeast Asia. Common throughout Myanmar in lowlands and low hills. **HABITAT AND HABITS** Often seen singly or rarely in pairs, in forest edges, scrub, riverine vegetation and plantations. Very shy and confined to thick vegetation, showing itself while sunning or scrambling among foliage. Usually in lowlands, but can occur in disturbed vegetation in hills. Call a prolonged series of deep booms. **STATUS** Common.

Green-billed Malkoha ▪ *Phaenicophaeus tristis* 50–60cm

DESCRIPTION Large, grey, and with very long, white-tipped tail; pale grey breast and

grey belly and vent; green bill and red skin around eye. **DISTRIBUTION** Widespread in Southeast Asia and eastern South Asia. Uncommon throughout Myanmar across plains and to 1,600m in surrounding hills. **HABITAT AND HABITS** Occurs in wide range of habitats, from mountain forests down to coastal mangroves, bamboo groves, orchards and plantations. Clambers inside thick bushes and clumps of vines in tree canopies, foraging for large insects in dense foliage around tree trunks. **STATUS** Uncommon.

Pied Cuckoo
■ *Clamator jacobinus* 31–34cm

DESCRIPTION Slim, with long tail and short, shaggy crest; black above and entirely white below, with white half-collar, small white patch on primaries, and white tail-tip. Juveniles duller than adults; charcoal and buff, not pure black and white. **DISTRIBUTION** Africa and South Asia to Indochina. Breeding migrant in Central and South Myanmar, occasionally on migration in South-west. **HABITAT AND HABITS** Dry, open woodland, tree plantations, orchards and scrub mostly in lowlands. Repeated clarion cries by male during breeding season. Known brood parasite of babblers, including the White-throated Babbler (p. 118). **STATUS** Uncommon.

Asian Koel ■ *Eudynamys scolopaceus* 39–46cm

DESCRIPTION Substantial long-tailed cuckoo with red iris. Male generally glossy black. Female mainly dark brown with spots on head and upperparts, and barred tail; light

brown underparts with dark brown streaks and bars. **DISTRIBUTION** Widespread in South and Southeast Asia. In Myanmar across plains and to 1,200m in surrounding hills. **HABITAT AND HABITS** Seen in coastal areas, plantations, and wooded gardens in towns and cities. Generally shy and confined to security of dense foliage, but loud, rising, repeated *Ko-el* (male) and shrill bubbling calls (female) betray its presence, especially in breeding season. Known brood parasite of crows, mynas and possibly orioles. **STATUS** Common.

Plaintive Cuckoo
■ *Cacomantis merulinus* 18–23.5cm

DESCRIPTION Slim, fairly long-tailed cuckoo with light grey head and upper breast; brown back and wings, and blackish tail with white bars on outer feathers visible in flight or more reliably when seen from below. Lower breast and belly peachy-rufous. Rufous-brown plumage form in female has black mottling on back, and black and white barring on belly. DISTRIBUTION Widespread in Southeast Asia and eastern South Asia. HABITAT AND HABITS Predominantly found in lowlands, in tall secondary woodland, old plantations and forest edges, sometimes in urban areas, occasionally reaching montane elevations. Best known by steadily rising call, a series of three-note phrases, *phee-sa-phee*, with emphasis on third note, ascending scale and becoming louder. Also descending series of 8–10 notes, quickening at the end. STATUS Common.

Common Cuckoo
■ *Cuculus canorus* 32–34cm

DESCRIPTION Male light grey, except for lower breast and belly that are pure white with distinct but narrow dark bars. Very similar **Himalayan Cuckoo** C. *saturatus* slightly smaller, darker yellow eye, with unbarred inner primary coverts, strongly barred in Common. **Lesser Cuckoo** C. *poliocephalus* smaller again, generally darker grey above and even more buffy below, migrating to and from East Africa, appearing later in spring than other cuckoos. DISTRIBUTION Breeding visitor in Central, West, North and East Myanmar; passage migrant in South-west Myanmar. HABITAT AND HABITS Resident above 600m, in broadleaved forest and tall secondary growth. Best identified by voice, the classic *Cuck-coo*. STATUS Uncommon.

Masked Finfoot ■ *Heliopais personatus* 43–55cm

DESCRIPTION Both sexes generally olive-brown but slightly darker on upperparts; iris yellow; bill large and yellow; feet greenish-yellow and webbed. Adult male has black throat and face with white line from back of eye. Female has white throat.

DISTRIBUTION Very limited in remote forests in Myanmar and Cambodia. **HABITAT AND HABITS** Encounters limited to individuals in preferred habitats of forested waterways, secluded pools and coastal Bangladesh, in mangroves. Very shy and secretive. Swims with head bobbing and usually keeps close to the water's edge and vegetation. **STATUS** Formerly throughout Myanmar; decreasing, with recent records limited to North.

Slaty-legged Crake
■ *Rallina eurizonoides* 21–25cm

DESCRIPTION Rufous-chestnut head and breast, sharply cut off from black- and white-barred belly; darker brown wings and back. Differs from similar but smaller **Red-legged Crake** *R. fasciata* by grey (not red) legs and eye-ring, and no white speckling on shoulder. **DISTRIBUTION** India and China to the Philippines and Java. East, Central and North Myanmar. **HABITAT AND HABITS** Found in dense vegetation along margins of freshwater swamps, streams, in forest edges and tall vegetation, but almost anywhere on migration, including gardens. Secretive but detected by clucking and drumming calls at night and dawn. **STATUS** Uncertain. Possibly breeding as well as migrant.

White-breasted Waterhen ■ *Amaurornis phoenicurus* 28–33cm

DESCRIPTION White face and breast, merging to rufous beneath tail, and dark back and wings, make species unmistakable. Sexes alike. **DISTRIBUTION** Widespread in South and Southeast Asia. Common throughout Myanmar across plains and to 1,200m in surrounding hills. **HABITAT AND HABITS** Commonly seen in rank vegetation and overgrown drains, and along roadsides in rural areas, sometimes flying up when disturbed. Adults may be accompanied by several half-grown, fluffy black chicks; pale breast plumage gradually appears as chicks grow. Utters monotonous single, piping note endlessly repeated, or chorus of grating and gurgling notes in which male and female participate, competing with neighbouring pairs. **STATUS** Common.

White-browed Crake ■ *Porzana cinerea* 20cm

DESCRIPTION Small, pale grey and buff rail, mottled brown and blackish on wings; grey breast; blackish and white stripes across face; stubby bill greenish-yellow with a little red at base; legs green. **DISTRIBUTION** Widespread from Southeast Asia to northern Australia. Confirmed in Myanmar in 2013, with birds known to breed in Mandalay and Indawgyi Lake. **HABITAT AND HABITS** Restricted to a few wetlands. Often clambers about just above the water's surface in dense floating vegetation, grass and reeds in freshwater lakes, ponds and ditches; secretive. **STATUS** Uncommon. Probably more widespread than currently known.

Grey-headed Swamphen ■ *Porphyrio poliocephalus* 38–50cm

DESCRIPTION Big, gaudy rail. Plumage deep purplish-blue, red bill, forehead and legs, and white below tail. In poor light can look merely blackish at a distance. Sexes alike.

DISTRIBUTION Populations through southern and Southeast Asia. North, Central and South Myanmar. **HABITAT AND HABITS** Occasionally seen in ones or twos in swampy habitat, where it feeds on succulent water plants, holding material in one foot and slicing it with the secateur-like bill. Nest a bowl of piled up weeds in dense vegetation in marsh. Utters a variety of loud, braying, chuckling and clattering notes in morning and evening, but secretive and falls silent and retreats into vegetation when approached. **STATUS** Uncommon.

Sarus Crane ■ *Grus antigone* 152–176cm;
Common Crane ■ *G. grus* 95–120cm

DESCRIPTION Sarus huge, and grey with bare red head and red legs in adult; juveniles have dirty buff head. Common large, and ashy-grey with black and white head and neck, and some red on crown. In both species elongated secondaries form bustle over tail when standing. **DISTRIBUTION** Sarus found South Asia, Myanmar and Cambodia, reintroduced to Thailand. Common Crane occurs from Europe to China. Migrant in North, Central and West Myanmar. **HABITAT AND HABITS** Forages in open grassland, especially in marshy areas remote from people, and in rice fields. Found singly or in small groups. Very wary and alert. **STATUS** Rare and declining resident (Sarus); uncommon non-breeding migrant (Common).

Sarus Crane

Common Crane

Lesser Adjutant ■ *Leptoptilos javanicus* 110–120cm

DESCRIPTION Large, grey and white wading bird with bare pink head and orange neck,

large, thick bill and long grey legs. **DISTRIBUTION** Only in a few remaining areas, in coastal Tenasserim, South, South-west, Central and North Myanmar. **HABITAT AND HABITS** Found singly or in pairs in wetlands, along rivers and in coastal mangroves, feeding on nearby mudflats. Omnivorous and occasionally scavenges carrion. **STATUS** Locally uncommon resident. Declining due to persecution and loss of habitat.

Painted Stork ■ *Mycteria leucocephala* 93–102cm

DESCRIPTION Large white wading bird with bare red head and thick, yellow decurved bill. Wings predominately black with white bands. Variable black breast-band, and bases of wings often suffused with pink, most easily seen while at rest. **DISTRIBUTION** Throughout South, Central and North Myanmar. **HABITAT AND HABITS** Occurs in large wetlands and rivers. Often feeds with Asian Openbills (opposite). Soars for long distances and often seen in small groups flying very high in the air. **STATUS** Uncommon visitor, presumed resident but nesting areas are still to be found.

Asian Openbill ■ *Anastomus oscitans* 81cm

DESCRIPTION Large, dull white wading bird, with white wings with black flight feathers. Bill specially formed with gap between upper and lower mandibles – used to manipulate large snails, its primary food. **DISTRIBUTION** Throughout Myanmar. **HABITAT AND HABITS** Wetlands, rivers and rice fields. **STATUS** Common. Seems to be increasing as persecution has reduced in recent years due to people understanding its benefits in removing invasive snails from their rice fields.

Asian Woollyneck ■ *Ciconia episcopus* 86–95cm

DESCRIPTION Large dark wading bird with dark cap and snowy-white neck, texture of feathers making it look like sheep's wool. Dark body and wings have purplish-blue sheen when seen in good light. Long, straight grey bill and long red legs. **DISTRIBUTION** Across South and Southeast Asia. Scattered locations through North, Central and South Myanmar. A few birds still breed at Hlawga Wildlife Park; otherwise seen on river between Bagan and Mandalay, and in wetlands of North. **HABITAT AND HABITS** Feeds in flooded fields and forested ponds; occasionally on large rivers and in rice fields with other wading birds. Often soars, usually in pairs. **STATUS** Uncommon and local resident.

Black-headed Ibis ■ *Threskiornis melanocephalus* 65–76cm;
Glossy Ibis ■ *Plegadis falcinellus* 48–66cm

DESCRIPTION Medium-sized wading bird. Black-headed white with bare black head, strongly decurved bill and long black legs. Glossy Ibis is brown with greenish-purple gloss on back and wings, fine white streaking on head and neck, long, decurved grey bill and long brown legs. May appear all dark in flight. **DISTRIBUTION** Throughout Myanmar at low densities. **HABITAT AND HABITS** Feed in wetlands, rice fields and occasionally in coastal areas on sand and mud. Nest communally, often in large concentrations of nesting egrets. **STATUS** Uncommon residents.

Black-headed Ibis

Glossy Ibis

Yellow Bittern ■ *Ixobrychus sinensis* 30–40cm;
Cinnamon Bittern ■ *I. cinnamomeus* 40–41cm

DESCRIPTION Small wading and clambering birds in reedbeds. Yellow has dull yellowish body, dark tail and wings, and black crown. Cinnamon chestnut-brown all over with tawny-yellowish belly. In flight, Yellow particoloured cream, brown and black; Cinnamon uniform in colour. Both have long yellow bill and legs. **DISTRIBUTION** Throughout Myanmar. **HABITAT AND HABITS** Skulk in reeds and rice fields; usually seen in flight, often low, just above vegetation. Occasionally perch in the open, freezing in the hopes that they will not be seen. **STATUS** Common residents.

Yellow Bittern

Cinnamon Bittern

Black-crowned Night-heron ■ *Nycticorax nycticorax* 56–65cm

DESCRIPTION Medium-sized wading bird, grey with dark back and black crown, dark bill and striking red eye. In breeding plumage has thin white plumes on crown. Juveniles completely different from adults, being covered in dark brown streaks. **DISTRIBUTION** Throughout Myanmar. Breeds in several areas around Yangon, including Hlawga Wildlife Park. Often seen flying over the city at dusk and heard croaking overhead in the middle of the night. **HABITAT AND HABITS** Primarily active at night. Often roosts in large numbers in trees close to wetland areas, leaving to forage at night in wetlands and rice fields. Nests in trees, often with other herons and egrets. **STATUS** Common resident.

Green-backed Heron ■ *Butorides striata* 35–48cm

DESCRIPTION Small wading bird, dull grey with dark green streaking; dark cap on dull green head, neck and back. Wings greenish with white feather edges. Long greenish bill and long yellow legs. Juveniles heavily streaked brown. **DISTRIBUTION** Cosmopolitan range, throughout Myanmar. **HABITAT AND HABITS** Usually found in comparatively wooded wetlands, often perched in trees or on branches next to stream or lake; also in coastal areas and mangroves. **STATUS** Common resident.

Chinese Pond Heron ▪ *Ardeola bacchus* 42–52cm;
Indian Pond Heron ▪ *A. grayii* 39–46cm

DESCRIPTION Non-breeding birds have light brown upperparts and wing-coverts; brown streaks from head to chest, and white underparts and wings; bill blackish with some yellow on lower mandible; legs yellow. When breeding, in Chinese head, throat, nape and breast rich chestnut; mantle black; underparts remain white; feet orange. In Indian head, throat, nape and breast browner; mantle maroon. Identification only reliable in breeding plumage. **DISTRIBUTION** Chinese through East and Southeast Asia, Indian through South Asia. Both overlap in Myanmar as breeders and winter visitors. **HABITAT AND HABITS** Found in mangroves, vegetated banks of rivers, lakes and reservoirs. Often solitary or in small, loose groups, sometimes mixed with other herons or egrets, or alone in dense vegetation. **STATUS** Common throughout Myanmar.

Chinese Pond Heron   *Indian Pond Heron*

Grey Heron
▪ *Ardea cinerea* 90–98cm

DESCRIPTION One of the largest herons in the region. Plumage generally grey; white on head, neck and underparts, and darker on mantle and wings. Broad black eye-stripe, primaries and head plume (may not be visible at times). White central stripe down front of neck bordered by irregular black streaks, and black patch on sides of body near bend of wing. Bill and legs yellow, brighter when breeding. **DISTRIBUTION** Widespread in Old World. Throughout Myanmar. **HABITAT AND HABITS** Found in any kind of shallow water; often seen along large rivers and wetlands. **STATUS** Common resident and winter visitor.

White-bellied Heron ■ *Ardea insignis* 127cm

DESCRIPTION Bigger and more heavily built than Grey or Purple Herons (opposite and below). Plumage overall rather uniform dark slaty-grey, but in good view shows narrow pale streaking on lower neck and breast, with white throat, belly and undertail-coverts. White belly contrasts with dark wings when seen in flight. **DISTRIBUTION** India to Nepal. In Myanmar now only in North; previously also Central, West and South. **HABITAT AND HABITS** Found in rivers and wetlands. Stand-and-wait fishing on banks. Occasionally nests far upriver. Very similar **Great-billed Heron** A. *sumatrana* tends to be more coastal in southern Myanmar mangroves. **STATUS** Resident in North. Declining, with less than 20 known individuals. Expansion of people and development have driven it to most remote and pristine remaining areas in Himalaya, which must remain wild for it to survive.

Purple Heron

■ *Ardea purpurea* 78–90cm

DESCRIPTION Almost same size as the Grey Heron (opposite) but slimmer. Plumage ashy-grey at base of neck, upper body and wings. Head and neck rufous with black stripe from base of gape down to belly. Cap black. Bill yellow with some black on upper mandible; feet light yellow. In flight, differs from Grey Heron by dark plumage, chestnut underwings and skinny appearance. **DISTRIBUTION** Widespread in Old World. Throughout Myanmar. **HABITAT AND HABITS** Associated with brackish and freshwater wetlands. Mainly solitary, often hunting quietly for fish in shallow waters by stalking and stabbing. Breeding colonies in lowlands, sometimes in trees with other herons and egrets, but often nests in thick vegetation on the ground. **STATUS** Uncommon resident.

Cattle Egret ▪ *Bubulcus ibis* 46–56cm;
Little Egret ▪ *Egretta garzetta* 55–65cm

DESCRIPTION Medium-sized white wading birds. Cattle has yellow legs and bill, and heavy jowls. Looks short necked and stubby compared to other egrets. In breeding season has bright ochre plumes on head, neck, breast and back. Little slimmer with dark legs, yellow feet and slender dark bill.

DISTRIBUTION Widespread in Old World. Throughout Myanmar. **HABITAT AND HABITS** Often found in drier habitats than other egrets and regularly associate with cattle and Water Buffalo. Can form large flocks when moving from fields to roosts at dawn and dusk. Little found more often along rivers and coasts than other egrets. Feeds actively, often making small dashes to chase after prey. **STATUS** Common residents.

Cattle Egret   *Little Egret*

Great Egret ▪ *Ardea alba* 80–104cm;
Intermediate Egret ▪ *A. intermedia* 56–72cm

DESCRIPTION Large white wading birds with dark legs and yellow bill. Intermediate easily confused with Great; differentiated by slightly smaller size, shorter neck giving it more upright stance, and obviously darker bill-tip. **DISTRIBUTION** Throughout Myanmar. All egrets nest colonially; often all four species together, with other waterbirds. Many nesting areas are near Buddhist temples, where they are protected from disturbance. **HABITAT AND HABITS** More often in wetlands and rivers than rice fields. **STATUS** Common residents.

Great Egret   *Intermediate Egret*

Pacific Reef-egret
■ *Egretta sacra* 58–66cm

DESCRIPTION Large coastal wading bird with proportionately rather short yellow legs and yellow bill. Two forms: white and dark greyish-blue. Has head and breast plumes when breeding. **DISTRIBUTION** Southern China through Southeast Asia to Australia, New Zealand and Polynesia. In Myanmar in small numbers along most coastlines. **HABITAT AND HABITS** Usually found feeding along coastal mud and rocks, especially among coastal reefs at low tide. Occurs singly or in pairs, never in large flocks. Does not occur inland. **STATUS** Uncommon resident.

Spot-billed Pelican
■ *Pelecanus philippensis* 127–152cm

DESCRIPTION Large white pelican, with dull pinkish bill with dark spots along top mandible. Usually seen soaring high overhead or feeding along large rivers or in big wetlands. Feeds by scooping fish into large pouch in bill. The water is strained out and the bird swallows the fish. **DISTRIBUTION** Across South and Southeast Asia. In Myanmar in North, Central and South. **HABITAT AND HABITS** Occurs in a variety of wetlands, especially large lakes and along larger rivers. Still not confirmed to breed in Myanmar, but could be travelling long distances as far away as Northeast India and Cambodia to feed. **STATUS** Uncommon visitor.

Little Cormorant ■ *Microcarbo niger* 51–56cm;
Great Cormorant ■ *Phalacrocorax carbo* 80–100cm

DESCRIPTION Little is smallest local cormorant, all black with pale streaking on head; small bill black when breeding, pale when not. Great almost double the bulk, all dark with white around face and throat, and yellow bill-base; white and yellow prominent and extensive when breeding. Juveniles of both pale brown, very different in size. **DISTRIBUTION** Throughout Myanmar. Great more common in North. **HABITAT AND HABITS** Both occur in freshwater and saline wetlands, typically in lowlands where they breed, but (especially Great) can venture far inland. Dive for fish and dry outspread wings when perched. **STATUS** Common.

Little Cormorant   *Great Cormorant*

Oriental Darter ■ *Anhinga melanogaster* 85–97cm

DESCRIPTION Large, slim black bird with small head, snake-like neck and pointed yellowish bill. Plumage generally black, with conspicuous pale streaks on wings, especially when sunning in the open. Head and neck brown with narrow white stripe running from gape down sides of neck. Flies with neck outstretched. **DISTRIBUTION** Uncommon in Myanmar. **HABITAT AND HABITS** Restricted to mostly remote inland freshwater swamps, lakes and rivers, and coastal forest, typically in lowlands, where it breeds. Dives for fish. When swimming, body slightly submerged below water, leaving only protruding head and thin neck showing; appears like a snake, giving it informal name 'snakebird'. Often seen sunning for long periods on exposed branches, with outstretched wings and tail, drying its waterlogged plumage. Roosts communally on bare trees near riverbanks. Frequents urban lakes around Yangon and Mandalay, as well as large wetlands at Inle Lake. **STATUS** Uncommon.

Great Thick-knee ■ *Esacus recurvirostris* 42–54cm

DESCRIPTION Large, sandy-coloured shorebird with very heavy black bill, black and white face-stripes, and dark bar on shoulder. In flight transforms into tricolour sandy, black and white bird with dark wing feathers and small white panel on inner primaries. **DISTRIBUTION** India to Southwest China. Scattered and patchy along main rivers in Myanmar, except Tenasserim, where replaced by very similar **Beach Thick-knee** *E. neglectus*. **HABITAT AND HABITS** Seen singly, or often in pairs, on sandy or shingle banks of large rivers and lakes, sometimes down to coastal mud or sand (where tracks show absence of hind-toe). Wild whistling calls when breeding and in flight. **STATUS** Locally uncommon. Restricted to least disturbed areas along major rivers in North and Central Myanmar. Declining due to increased human disturbance on riverine sandbanks.

Ibisbill ■ *Ibidorhyncha struthersii* 39–41cm

DESCRIPTION Large wading bird with sandy-grey wings and back, narrow black breast-band separating grey neck from white belly, and black face (much reduced in juveniles). Red legs and red, downcurved sickle bill. **DISTRIBUTION** Mountains and plateaus of Central Asia, including North Myanmar. **HABITAT AND HABITS** Seen singly or in pairs, wading in shallow rocky rivers, in hills and mountains, probing between and below boulders and pebbles for aquatic insects. **STATUS** Uncommon winter visitor in far North Myanmar.

Breeding   *Non-breeding*

Black-winged Stilt
■ *Himantopus himantopus* 35–40cm

DESCRIPTION Slim and elegant, with long pink legs and slender bill; head, neck and underparts white with variable dusky markings on crown, face, neck; wings black in adults, dusky in juveniles. **DISTRIBUTION** Resident in most of temperate Old World, migrating to tropics. **HABITAT AND HABITS** Small flocks occur in wet rice fields, open marshes and occasionally near the sea. Nests on muddy banks of lakes or on wet vegetation. **STATUS** Uncommon resident. Often trapped for food in wetlands around Mandalay.

Little Ringed Plover ■ *Charadrius dubius* 14–17cm

DESCRIPTION Small plover with pale forehead, throat and collar, complete dark breast-band, and white underparts; small bill all dark, pale ring of skin around eye, and legs

pale olive to pink. Coming into breeding plumage, contrasts heightened, with black face-mask distinct, and eye-ring clear yellow. **DISTRIBUTION** Resident through subarctic and temperate Eurasia to Middle East, Sri Lanka, and the Philippines to New Guinea. **HABITAT AND HABITS** Primarily found in freshwater habitats near temporary pools, on short grass and open ground, mud, ploughed farmland and rice fields; occasionally on intertidal mud. Often wanders separately over feeding habitat, flying up to form flock when disturbed. **STATUS** Common resident; most regularly seen small plover across Myanmar.

River Lapwing ■ *Vanellus duvaucelii* 29.5–31cm

DESCRIPTION Black legs, and black crown, face and throat diagnostic. Large white patch on hind-face and neck, separated from white belly by narrow, sandy breast-band; sandy-brown wings and back. In flight, narrow white band (edged black) separates dark primaries from sandy inner wing. **DISTRIBUTION** India to southern China and Indochina. Throughout lowland Myanmar in suitable habitat, but scattered and local. **HABITAT AND HABITS** Found along larger rivers in lowlands, mostly below 600m, on sandbanks and immediately adjacent farmland. High-pitched, piping, two-syllable calls when in flight. **STATUS** Uncommon resident.

Grey-headed Lapwing ■ *Vanellus cinereus* 34–37cm;
Red-wattled Lapwing ■ *V. indicus* 32–35cm

DESCRIPTION Both bigger than the River Lapwing (above). Grey-headed has pale ashy head and neck, dark breast-band, and (in flight) white secondaries. Red-wattled has black head, neck and upper breast, white ear-patch, red skin around eye to bill-base, and (in flight) narrow white wing-band not edged in black. Both have yellow legs. **DISTRIBUTION** Grey-headed in north China and Japan; Red-wattled from West Asia to India and Southwest China. In Myanmar, occurs anywhere in lowlands with suitable habitat. **HABITAT AND HABITS** Both found in rice fields and marshes; less often along rivers. Grey-headed utters simple, two-syllable calls; Red-wattled gives lovely rolling, 3–4-syllable cadence, *kree-dee-DEER* or *kree-de-dee-DEER*, often repeated monotonously, including when flushed.. **STATUS** Uncommon non-breeding visitor (Grey-headed); locally common resident (Red-wattled).

Grey-headed Lapwing

Red-wattled Lapwing

Pheasant-tailed Jacana ■ *Hydrophasianus chirurgus* 39–58cm

DESCRIPTION Slim, elegant particoloured bird, with white face and wings, yellow hindneck and black underparts when breeding, and arched tail streamers. White underparts and dull mealy-brown wings, dark neck-stripe and short tail in juveniles and when not breeding. In flight, white and black wings with central brown panel on back. **DISTRIBUTION** India to Central China and the Philippines, migrating south just into Indonesia. Throughout Myanmar patchily in any suitable habitat in lowlands. **HABITAT AND HABITS** Found on and among water plants (water lilies, Water Hyacinth) on ponds and lakes, to 1,000m. On migration in similar habitat or in mangroves. **STATUS** Resident and migrant. Scarce to locally common.

Juvenile

Non-breeding

Breeding

Bronze-winged Jacana ■ *Jacana metopidius indicus* 28–31cm

DESCRIPTION Short-tailed, all-dark jacana with entirely black head, neck and underparts, white eye-stripe and short, robust yellow bill. Juvenile like non-breeding Pheasant-tailed Jacana (above), but has dark hindneck, lacks dark stripe down neck to breast, and upperparts darker brown, not scaly. **DISTRIBUTION** India to southern China, discontinuously to Java. Throughout Myanmar lowlands. **HABITAT AND HABITS** Found on and among dense waterplants on ponds and lakes, to 1,000m, where it breeds. More secretive, less vocal and less sociable than Pheasant-tailed. **STATUS** Locally common or uncommon resident.

Eurasian Curlew ■ *Numenius arquata* 50–60cm;
Whimbrel ■ *N. phaeopus* 40–46cm

DESCRIPTION Large waders, mottled, spotted and barred with brown and buff. Whimbrel best recognized by dark lateral stripes on crown with central pale line, and long, curved bill. Usually shows white rump in flight, but some birds are from dark-rumped population. Scarcer curlew also white rumped but bigger, no bold crown-stripes and much longer bill. **DISTRIBUTION** Breeds in Arctic and subarctic northern hemisphere; migrant south to Africa and Australasia. **HABITAT AND HABITS** Typically on coastal mudflats fronting mangroves, sometimes in big flocks, probing mud or wet sand for worms. Utters a clear trill, often when taking flight. Curlew has more musical cry heard at any time

Whimbrel

of year. **STATUS** Uncommon migrant and non-breeding visitor, rarely seen along large rivers or crossing mountains in north on migration.

Eurasian Curlew

Whimbrel

Red-necked Stint ■ *Calidris ruficollis* 13–16cm;
Long-toed Stint ■ *C. subminuta* 14–16cm

DESCRIPTION Tiny waders, typically seen in non-breeding plumage. Red-necked has washed out appearance; mottled grey above, white below with pale grey sides to upper breast, and short black bill and legs. Long-toed has longer neck, longer, slimmer bill with paler lower mandible, yellow legs, and upperparts and sides of breast slightly browner. **DISTRIBUTION** Breed in Central and Eastern Siberia, migrating to South and Southeast Asia and Australasia. **HABITAT AND HABITS** Red-necked more characteristic of coastal mudflats and wet sand, in the open; Long-toed more often on inland fresh water, among vegetation. **STATUS** Common migrant and non-breeding visitor.

Red-necked Stint

Long-toed Stint

Spoon-billed Sandpiper ■ *Calidris pygmeus* 14–16cm

DESCRIPTION Tiny wader. Like stints but whiter below, with more white on eyebrow and forehead. Spoon-shaped bill-tip is clinching feature. Most similar to Red-necked Stint (p.

45), but slightly darker grey above in non-breeding plumage, and often with slightly more erect posture. **DISTRIBUTION** Breeds in far eastern Siberia; winters from southern China through Southeast Asia, Bangladesh and eastern India. Much of remaining population winters in Gulf of Mottama and along Rakhine and Ayeyarwady coasts on offshore sandbanks that are not easily accessed. Most easily seen on sandbanks off Ayeyawardy Delta and along Mon State coast near Mawlamyine. **HABITAT AND HABITS** Occurs on coastal mudflats and wet sand. Uses expanded bill-tip to sweep or dibble for food. Usually seen singly; hard to spot among flocks of other small jostling waders. **STATUS** Rare winter visitor.

Common Sandpiper ■ *Actitis hypoleucos* 19–21cm

DESCRIPTION Small wader with pale grey-brown upperparts; white below with

distinctive brown patch on each side of upper breast; pale brow and eye-ring. Dark bill and olive legs. In flight, white wing-bar and white sides to narrow brown rump. **DISTRIBUTION** Breeds across Palearctic and winters throughout Africa, Asia and Australasia. In Myanmar potentially found in any wetland, usually singly or in small groups. **HABITAT AND HABITS** Usually alone or in pairs. Abundant but thinly distributed in many habitats, including coasts, wet rice fields, rivers, ditches and even concrete-lined drains in towns, teetering along with bobbing tail. Utters shrill, piping call when flushed, while flying low over water on bowed wings. **STATUS** Common migrant and winter visitor.

Common Greenshank ■ *Tringa nebularia* 30–35cm

DESCRIPTION Fairly large wader. Slim, light grey above and whitish below, with long dark bill and greenish legs. In flight, shows wedge of white from rump to back, but no white wing-bar. In breeding plumage, face, upper breast and back more spotted and mottled. **DISTRIBUTION** Resident across northern temperate Eurasia from Europe to Siberia, migrating south to tropical Africa, Southwest, South and Southeast Asia, as far as the Philippines, Australia and New Zealand. **HABITAT AND HABITS** Common migrant on mudflats, as well as inland in wet rice fields, and along rivers or marshes. Numbers increase in October and decline markedly in March, but like many wader species 1–2 birds can be found in almost any month. **STATUS** Common migrant and winter visitor.

Wood Sandpiper ■ *Tringa glareola* 19–23cm;
Green Sandpiper ■ *T. ochropus* 21–24cm

DESCRIPTION Wood a small, lively wader, dark ashy-grey with distinctive pale brow and mottled back and wings; in flight, barred tail and squared off white rump does not extend in wedge up back, dark bill and yellowish legs. Green with similar pattern but dark, often showing more contrast between back and wings and broad white rump. **DISTRIBUTION** Both breed in temperate and high-latitude Europe and Asia, wintering south into tropics. **HABITAT AND HABITS** Wood very common in freshwater marshes, wet rice fields and in mangroves. Often mixes with many other waders. Green more often in more wooded wetlands, and often along small streams with forested edges. **STATUS** Common across many habitats, and often seen in small groups in rice fields (Wood); uncommon and usually seen singly (Green).

Wood Sandpiper   *Green Sandpiper*

Oriental Pratincole ■ *Glareola maldivarum* 23–25cm;
Small Pratincole ■ *G. lactea* 16–19cm

DESCRIPTION Sandy brown above and paler below, with short legs, Oriental has cream throat outlined with black in adult, long, dark wings with chestnut lining, short, forked tail and white rump. Small is smaller, far paler sandy-grey, with dark wing-tips and large white wing-panels seen in flight. **DISTRIBUTION** Oriental breeds across East and Southeast Asia, and winters in north-west and west Australia. Breeding visitor in Myanmar, January–August, often occurring in large flocks. Small found across Indian subcontinent and mainland Southeast Asia. Also breeds in first half of year, during peak of dry season when riverine sandbanks are most extensive. **HABITAT AND HABITS** Oriental often seen standing on ploughed fields or foraging for insects in flight over cultivation. Small characteristic of sand and pebble banks on large rivers, or edges of lakes; rarely on coast. Both form large flocks when not breeding, feeding at dusk and dawn. **STATUS** Locally common to abundant.

Oriental Pratincole

Small Pratincole

Brown-headed Gull ■ *Larus brunnicephalus* 41–45cm

DESCRIPTION Medium-sized pale gull with darks smudges around and behind pale eye. In flight shows black wing-tips with white spot ('mirror'). Blackish-brown head of breeding plumage usually seen in spring. Larger size, pale eye and wing-tip pattern distinguish it from the **Black-headed Gull** *L. ridibundus* well known in many countries. **DISTRIBUTION** Breeds across Tibetan Plateau and Central Asia, migrating into Indian subcontinent and mainland Southeast Asia. **HABITAT AND HABITS** Found in coastal wetlands, rivers, large lakes like Inle and Indawgyi, often in quite large flocks. **STATUS** Common in favoured habitats, where it often congregates when fed by visitors.

Breeding

Non-breeding

Pallas's Gull ■ *Larus ichthyaetus* 59–72cm

DESCRIPTION Large, heavily built gull, with yellow legs and heavy yellow bill with darker tip or subterminal band. When standing, wing-tips black with series of white spots; in flight, primary feathers largely white with limited black subterminal markings. **DISTRIBUTION** Breeds in Central Asia and migrates to Middle East, and South and Southeast Asia. **HABITAT AND HABITS** Found along coast, on mudflats and sand, sometimes upriver, giving deep, gruff calls and scavenging or stealing food. **STATUS** Uncommon winter visitor seen along large rivers and concentrated at river-mouth mudflats.

Whiskered Tern ■ *Chlidonias hybrida* 23–29cm

DESCRIPTION Breeding birds sport red bill and legs; black crown and nape; underparts and mantle grey. Non-breeding birds generally greyish; forehead and sides of head white; bill and streak behind eye black. **DISTRIBUTION** Breeds across Eurasia and winters in Africa, Middle East, and South and Southeast Asia. **HABITAT AND HABITS** Commonly seen along coastal and inland wetlands across Myanmar during migration periods, when it moves to breeding areas in northern Asia. Congregates, hunts for food by making shallow plunges or skimming low over water. **STATUS** Common winter visitor.

River Tern ■ *Sterna aurantia* 38–46cm

DESCRIPTION Medium to large tern with light grey upperparts, black crown streaked grey on forehead, and heavy yellow bill with black tip. Juveniles have pale eyebrow,

blackish scaling on back and wings, and dark wing-line along tips of primaries. **DISTRIBUTION** Indian subcontinent to Southwest China. In Myanmar, now limited to larger rivers. **HABITAT AND HABITS** Freshwater bird, found along large rivers or sometimes lakes, usually in lowlands, sometimes to 1,200m. **STATUS** Rapidly declining and almost gone from Mekong basin. Still more than 100 pairs on Chindwin River, with smaller numbers along Ayeyarwady. Population has crashed due to increased disturbance from human activities along river sandbanks where it breeds.

Black-bellied Tern ■ *Sterna acuticauda* 32–35cm

DESCRIPTION Medium-sized tern with delicate orange bill, black crown and, in breeding plumage only, grey breast grading into black belly. **DISTRIBUTION** Indian subcontinent to Southwest China. Formerly widespread in Myanmar but now very local. **HABITAT AND HABITS** Freshwater tern, seen along rivers and sometimes at lakes in lowlands. Gives clear, piping call in flight. **STATUS** Already extirpated from Mekong River and barely hanging on, with seven known pairs remaining on Ayeyarwady River. Population has crashed due to increased disturbance from human activities along river sandbanks where it breeds.

Black-naped Tern ▪ *Sterna sumatrana* 30–35cm;
Greater Crested Tern ▪ *Thalasseus bergii* 43–53cm

DESCRIPTION Black-naped an elegant tern, with mainly white plumage with black line around nape and deeply forked tail; slender black bill. Greater Crested bulkier, grey above, with orange-yellow bill, and black crown ending in short, shaggy black crest. **DISTRIBUTION** Tropical waters of Indian and eastern Pacific Oceans. Along Myanmar coast most likely to be found in Rakhine and Mergui Archipelago. **HABITAT AND HABITS** Congregate in small groups, at times with other terns, either at offshore rocky outcrops where they nest, or at resting points on rocks, buoys or fishing stakes, flying low over sea and stooping to take small fish and prawns. **STATUS** Uncommon.

Black-naped Tern

Greater Crested Tern

Barn Owl ▪ *Tyto alba* 34–36cm;
Australian Grass-owl ▪ *T. longimembris* 35–40cm

DESCRIPTION Quite easily recognized owls with pale, heart-shaped faces with buffy rim. Throat and underparts white; head, upperparts and tail buffy with small whitish spots; legs long. Barn Owl paler, with whiter face. Grass-owl has dark smudges around eyes, and darker wings and back. **DISTRIBUTION** Barn Owl nearly global. Grass-owl in temperate and tropical Asia with closely related form in Africa. **HABITAT AND HABITS** Nocturnal, occurring in rural agricultural land. Grass-owl often in dry grassland with scattered trees, sometimes roosting on the ground. Barn Owl often in more urban areas, nesting and roosting in old buildings, and feeding on the numerous rats. Barn Owl usually only active late at night, Grass-owl also feeds at dusk, both can occasionally be flushed by day. **STATUS** Barn Owl found in Yangon, Mandalay and other large towns. Grass-owl much more restricted – often in large areas of grassland, around abandoned rice fields and on large sand islands in big rivers.

Barn Owl

Australian Grass-owl

Collared Owlet ■ *Glaucidium brodiei* 16cm

DESCRIPTION Very small, round-headed owl with yellow eyes. Barred brown and black plumage with plentiful white markings on breast and belly; like the Asian Barred Owlet

(below) but much smaller, and more speckled than barred. Nape dark buff with two dark, eye-like marks. **DISTRIBUTION** Across Himalaya, southern China and mainland Southeast Asia. Uncommon in hills and mountains across Myanmar. **HABITAT AND HABITS** Found in middle storey of tall forests, in hills to 3,100m. Often detected by day by distinctive, repeated *poop de-poop poop* call. Heard calling in middle of the day and regularly mobbed by smaller birds when doing so. **STATUS** Uncommon resident.

Asian Barred Owlet ■ *Glaucidium cuculoides* 21–23cm;
Spotted Owlet ■ *Athene brama* 20–21cm

DESCRIPTION Very like the Collared Owlet (above) but considerably bigger, upperparts more barred than speckled and lacks dark spots on nape. Spotted intermediate in size, greyer brown, more regularly spotted grey-brown below, without heavy white splashes of Collared or Asian Barred, but with dark bar between face and breast. **DISTRIBUTION** Asian Barred across Himalayan foothills and most of southern China and mainland Southeast Asia. Spotted restricted to dry forests from Iran through Indian subcontinent and mainland Southeast Asia. **HABITAT AND HABITS** Asian Barred seen in wooded country, at night and sometimes by day, giving tremulous bubbling call that fades in and fades out at end. Spotted in more open country, cultivation and villages with scattered trees, giving varied high-pitched, screeching calls. **STATUS** The most common owl in forested areas (Asian Barred); throughout drier lowlands, regularly in temples at Bagan and in parks and temples in Yangon and Mandalay (Spotted).

Asian Barred Owlet

Spotted Owlet

Oriental Scops-owl
■ *Otus sunia* 19cm

DESCRIPTION Small, rufous-brown owl with rufous and grey forms, short ear-tufts, speckled back, mottled white scapular line and dark streaks on forehead, crown and belly. Eyes yellow. **DISTRIBUTION** Across Himalayan foothills, most of eastern and southern China, and mainland Southeast Asia, with migrant and resident populations. **HABITAT AND HABITS** Keeps to tall secondary woodland, tree plantations, well-wooded gardens, and less commonly undisturbed forests, hunting for beetles, cockroaches, crickets, small lizards and other small vertebrates at night. Call is *toik, toik, toik*, rhythmic and repeated at regular short intervals. More often heard than seen. **STATUS** Uncommon.

Himalayan Owl ■ *Strix nivicolum* 43cm

DESCRIPTION Medium-sized owl with grey, buff and brown mottling, streaked below with darker cross-bars, and pale tips to scapulars and wing-coverts. Dark eyes, and diagonal pale 'eyebrows' extending over crown. Mid-grey and dark rufous plumage phases. **DISTRIBUTION** Across Himalaya, much of South and eastern China, to northern Korea and uplands of Myanmar and Vietnam. **HABITAT AND HABITS** Found in forests, both broadleaved and evergreen, in seemingly narrow-elevation band in mountains, at about 2,450–3,100m. Utters loud, deep, two-note hoot. **STATUS** Rare owl in forested mountains of North and West Myanmar.

Brown Fish-owl
■ *Ketupa zeylonensis* 49–54cm

DESCRIPTION Large, rich buffy-brown owl, with yellow eyes and droopy ear-tufts giving somewhat flat-crowned appearance. Warm buff below with narrow dark streaks and narrower cross-bars; heavily mottled above, with whitish and dark markings on wing-coverts. **DISTRIBUTION** Across Indian subcontinent and mainland Southeast Asia. The most regularly found large owl in Myanmar, often perched along forested rivers in predictable and well-known roosts. **HABITAT AND HABITS** Occurs in sparse tree cover in lowlands, in evergreen and semi-evergreen forests, especially near streams or rivers. Gives quick, three-note hoot, with third note virtually suppressed; also wild, screaming laughter. **STATUS** Uncommon resident.

Osprey ■ *Pandion haliaetus* 55cm

DESCRIPTION Medium-sized raptor with brown upperparts and tail. Head white with prominent brown/black eye-stripe. Short crest not always visible. Underparts and legs white with brown patches on chest. Iris yellow. **DISTRIBUTION** Global, breeding in temperate and subtropical regions, and wintering in tropical areas. Across Myanmar. **HABITAT AND HABITS** Seen along sea coasts, large rivers, inland natural and man-made wetlands, such as reservoirs, usually in flight. Feeds primarily on fish, caught by spectacular dives into the water, before emerging and taking off from the water's surface with prey in talons. **STATUS** Uncommon. Seen over any large lake or river during migration.

Black-winged Kite ■ *Elanus caeruleus* 32cm

DESCRIPTION Elegant, fairly small raptor. Light grey crown and darker grey upperparts, with black primaries. Face and underparts white to cream or pearly-grey. Bill black, iris red, black eyebrows and yellow legs. **DISTRIBUTION** Africa, south Eurasia, India and South China through Southeast Asia to New Guinea. Throughout

Myanmar. **HABITAT AND HABITS** Raptor of open country and agricultural areas such as rice fields, farmland and grassland. Often seen hovering in search of reptiles and rodents by day, but also uses utility poles as hunting perches. **STATUS** Common in farmland in lowlands and middle hills.

Oriental Honey-buzzard ■ *Pernis ptilorhynchus* 55–65cm

DESCRIPTION Medium-large raptor with variable individual plumages. In flight shows longish, proportionally small, pigeon-like head, long, square-cut tail with 2–3 dark bands, and long wings with numerous dark bands on undersurface. Upperparts brown to chocolate or blackish; underparts cinnamon to white with highly variable number of streaks and barring. **DISTRIBUTION** Migrant population from temperate Northeast Asia from Siberia to Japan and northern China; resident in India, southern China and Southeast Asia to Greater Sundas. Across Myanmar. **HABITAT AND HABITS** Favours forests and forest edges, as well as plantations and other wooded areas. Feeds on honeybee and wasp larvae by raiding their nests. Also takes small vertebrate prey, as well as chickens in villages opportunistically. Usually single or in pairs, but often forms small groups when northern races migrate through the country. **STATUS** One of the largest raptors regularly seen in Myanmar.

Crested Serpent-eagle ■ *Spilornis cheela* 54cm

DESCRIPTION Medium-sized, generally brownish raptor with short, bunchy crest (not always visible when perched). Upperparts greyish-brown; underparts lighter brown with

small white spots on breast, belly and carpals. Head darker brown, almost black in some individuals. Cere, iris and feet yellow; bill grey. Immatures mottled brown, with more white than adults. **DISTRIBUTION** India to South China; Southeast Asia to Greater Sundas. Across Myanmar. **HABITAT AND HABITS** Often heard or seen in various habitats such as rice fields, farmland and grassland. Usually solitary. At times seen perched on vantage points such as bare trees. Diet mainly snakes, lizards, some birds and small mammals. Regularly heard whistling, flying high overhead. **STATUS** Common, often in scrubby and forested habitats.

White-rumped Vulture ■ *Gyps bengalensis* 75–85cm

DESCRIPTION Bare pinkish-brown head and long neck separated from all-dark grey body and wings by white ruff. White rump, and very broad wings all dark above; black body and white wing lining seen in flight from below. Juveniles browner than adults, streaked below, with wing lining a little paler,

and narrow dark line along leading edge of wing; difficult to tell from **Himalayan Griffon** G. *himalayensis*. **DISTRIBUTION** Formerly across Indian subcontinent and mainland Southeast Asia. Once very common across Myanmar but now only two tiny populations – one near Indawgyi Lake in Kachin State and another east of Inle Lake in Shan State. **HABITAT AND HABITS** Favours dry, rather open country in lowlands and occasionally hills. Uses thermals to soar to spot carrion. Tree-nesting. **STATUS** Restricted and declining resident.

Black Eagle

■ *Ictinaetus malaiensis* 65–80cm

DESCRIPTION Large and very long-winged; tips of primaries extend beyond tail when perched. Shows very big, broad wings in flight. Virtually black all over; tail with slightly paler bars. Juveniles dark brown with paler barring on undersides of wings and tail. **DISTRIBUTION** South, Southeast and East Asia, to Sulawesi and Indonesian islands. Hills and mountains across Myanmar. **HABITAT AND HABITS** Typically seen soaring long distances over forest canopy, seeking squirrels and other arboreal vertebrate prey. Usually over montane forests, though extends down hill slopes and into lowlands. **STATUS** Uncommon resident.

Eastern Marsh-harrier ■ *Circus spilonotus* 48–56cm;
Pied Harrier ■ *C. melanoleucos* 43–46cm

DESCRIPTION Largely grey male Marsh streaked on neck and breast, and scalloped on back. Smaller male Pied reveals black breast, black wing-tips and dark grey back in flight. Female and juveniles brown, streaked on neck and below, thin white rump, with plain underwings and rufous-brown thighs in Marsh, barred underwing and whitish streaky thighs in Pied. **DISTRIBUTION** Breeds in eastern Eurasia and winters across southern China, Southeast Asia and Greater Sundas. In Myanmar, often in reasonable numbers in Bagan, Indawgyi and Inle Lakes. **HABITAT AND HABITS** Buoyant flight over marshes, rice fields and open grassland, seeking small mammal prey. Pied to more than 2,000m, Marsh to about 1,000m; occasionally together at communal roost sites with uncommon harriers, including the very similar **Western Marsh-harrier** *C. aeruginosus*. **STATUS** The two most common harriers across Myanmar during winter.

Eastern Marsh-harrier

Pied Harrier

Crested Goshawk
■ *Accipiter trivirgatus* 30–45cm

DESCRIPTION More heavily built than sparrowhawks. Adult has dark head, dark brown back and wings, and longish tail crossed by four broad dark bars; throat white with blackish stripe down centre, upper breast broadly streaked and lower breast barred brown. Crest inconspicuous. Immatures paler overall, and sparsely mottled brown below. In flight, banded tail and wings, with wing-tip showing six feathers. **DISTRIBUTION** South and Southeast Asia to Borneo and the Philippines. Tall forests across Myanmar; most often seen soaring overhead. **HABITAT AND HABITS** Forest bird, in lowlands and reaching well into montane elevations. Seen high overhead in thermals, over forest canopy or perched in middle or upper storey. Prey consists of small vertebrates. **STATUS** Uncommon resident.

Shikra ■ *Accipiter badius* 30–36cm

DESCRIPTION Pale grey, broad-winged hawk with washed out grey head, wings and tail, dark stripe down throat-centre, and closely barred, orange-buff underparts. In flight, extreme tips of wings dark, and four (male) or five (female) dark bands visible on underside of tail. Juveniles brown, streaked below, with five dark tail-bands. **DISTRIBUTION** Across subtropical and tropical Old World drier forests. Common small raptor in most lowland areas in Myanmar. **HABITAT AND HABITS** Found in dry deciduous and semi-evergreen forests and agricultural land, from lowlands to 1,600m, hunting birds in open areas. **STATUS** Common resident.

Male

Female

White-bellied Sea-eagle ■ *Haliaeetus leucogaster* 70–85cm

DESCRIPTION Large raptor with white head, underparts and tail. Dark grey upperparts and wings. Bill grey, iris brown/black, legs light yellow. Tail wedged, visible in flight. Immatures in various stages of mottled brown. **DISTRIBUTION** India and Southeast Asia, to Australia. In Myanmar, along West and Tenasserim coast. **HABITAT AND HABITS** Frequents coastal wetlands and even large inland wetlands such as large rivers and reservoirs. Feeds mainly on fish. Hunts by soaring and circling over waterbodies before swooping down to catch fish near the water's surface. Builds large nest on tall canopy trees or man-made structures such as telecommunications towers. Pairs very vocal. **STATUS** Uncommon resident.

Lesser Fish-eagle ■ *Icthyophaga humilis* 50–68cm

DESCRIPTION Light grey above and below, becoming browner on breast till sharp cut-off to white belly and undertail-coverts. In flight, wings grey with black flight feathers seen from above; all-dark wings seen from below, with white belly showing well. In all plumages, dark tail (contra **Grey-headed Fish-eagle** *I. ichthyaetus*, which shows white tail with distinct black terminal band). **DISTRIBUTION** Across South, Southeast Asia and Indonesia. Mostly in North, West and Tenasserim, Myanmar. **HABITAT AND HABITS** Occurs along forested rivers in lowlands, waiting on branch to spot fish below, and retreating ahead of passing boats. **STATUS** Declining. Only found in remaining areas of forested rivers.

Black Kite ■ *Milvus migrans* 45–65cm

DESCRIPTION Dark brown with blue-grey cere and feet; faintly streaked lighter below. Long-winged, and long, square to slightly fork-tipped tail seen well in slow, graceful flight that includes much soaring.

DISTRIBUTION Palaearctic from mainland Europe to Japan and Indochina, wintering south to Borneo; and from Sulawesi to Australasia. In Myanmar, a few pairs still breed around Yangon and often roost on islands in Inya Lake. Regularly seen in Mandalay and Bagan, often roosting on sandbanks in rivers. More numerous migratory race from Northeast Asia passes through same areas. **HABITAT AND HABITS** Soars over lowlands; often several wheel high in thermals, seeking carrion and small mammals, frogs, insects and occasionally birds, or fish waste along coast. In selected safe spots such as islands, communal roosts can be formed. **STATUS** Uncommon resident breeding across lowlands.

White-eyed Buzzard
■ *Butastur teesa* 42cm

DESCRIPTION As large as a buzzard but lightly built; dark grey-brown with paler panel across wing-coverts and more rufous rump and tail. Throat whitish with dark median streak in adults. Staring pale eye. In flight, all dark with rufous tail above, and buffy underparts, buff wing-lining and whitish flight feathers from below, with darker wing-tips. **DISTRIBUTION** Iran across Indian subcontinent to Myanmar, where mostly seen near Mandalay and Bagan. **HABITAT AND HABITS** Found in dry lowlands, open country with scattered trees and cultivation, often allowing good views when perched. **STATUS** Uncommon raptor found regularly in dry zone.

Japanese Buzzard ■ *Buteo japonicus* 39–45cm

DESCRIPTION Mottled brown above and below; back and wing-coverts with paler fringes; streaked and barred dark brown on pale breast and belly. Tail has several faint cross-bars and one heavier subterminal dark bar. In flight, pale, lightly barred flight feathers tipped darker, forming dark rear rim to wing, with darker underwing-coverts rufous or mottled brown. Various colour phases (pale, rufous, dark) and ages make distinction from the **Himalayan Buzzard** B. *refectus* challenging. **DISTRIBUTION** Central Asia from about 100°E to Japan, wintering into Southeast Asia. Usually most commonly found in North and Central Myanmar. **HABITAT AND HABITS** Seen soaring over open country or resting on tree or fencepost. **STATUS** The regular wintering buzzard in Myanmar.

Red-headed Trogon
■ *Harpactes erythrocephalus* 33cm

DESCRIPTION Large trogon with diagnostic red head in male and cinnamon in female. Both have reddish underparts with white 'crescent' on chest (sometimes hidden between feathers), cinnamon back and upper tail, and black wings with whitish stripes on wing-coverts. **DISTRIBUTION** Resident from Himalaya to South China, Southeast Asia and Sumatra. Hill forests throughout Myanmar, especially North, West, East and Tenasserim. **HABITAT AND HABITS** Prefers hill forests at 700m. Usually seen in middle storey. Generally unobtrusive. Frugivore recorded participating in birdwaves. **STATUS** Uncommon resident.

Great Hornbill
■ *Buceros bicornis* 110–120cm

DESCRIPTION One of the bulkiest hornbills, easily recognized by pied appearance, with head and white parts of plumage often stained yellow by oils from preen gland. Male and female alike, except for eye colour (red in male, white in female). Casque tends to be larger in male, with black trimmings. **DISTRIBUTION** Resident in parts of India, Bangladesh and Myanmar to Southwest China, and south to Sumatra. Healthy populations survive in North and Tenasserim, Myanmar, but hunting has depleted population in West and East. **HABITAT AND HABITS** Found in lowland and hill forests from sea level to about 1,300m. Typically in pairs, but sometimes gathers in larger groups at good food sources such as heavily fruiting fig trees. Call a loud barking, with male and female alternating, when perched or in flight. **STATUS** Uncommon and declining resident.

Austen's Brown Hornbill
■ *Anorrhinus austeni* 74cm

DESCRIPTION Small, dark hornbill with grey-brown crown, nape, back, wings and tail, but whitish throat and neck-sides, and breast gradually showing rufous flush towards belly. Whitish tips to tail feathers and secondaries show in flight. Ivory-yellow bill with small casque. **DISTRIBUTION** North, East and West Myanmar. **HABITAT AND HABITS** Often in noisy gangs, following one another from tree to tree in evergreen forests and secondary woodland, in lowlands to 1,800m. **STATUS** Uncommon or locally common resident. Threatened due to deforestation.

Oriental Pied Hornbill ■ *Anthracoceros albirostris* 68–70cm

DESCRIPTION Small hornbill and one of most common species, with black head, neck and wings, and white lower breast and outer-tail feathers. Bare, pale skin patches around eye and gape. Bill and casque ivory coloured, with obscure dark patches in female, and fewer but more defined, intense black marks in male. **DISTRIBUTION** Resident from India to Southwest China and throughout Southeast Asia to Sumatra, Borneo and Java. Throughout Myanmar. **HABITAT AND HABITS** Occurs in lowland forest edges, mangroves and along rivers, sometimes in plantations and gardens, seldom above 1,000m. Like other hornbills, nests in tree cavities. Female sealed in with mud except for narrow slit through which male passes food to her and offspring. Exciting recent work with cameras and satellite tracking has revealed many details of the breeding cycle, including an astonishing range of animal prey. **STATUS** Common resident.

Rufous-necked Hornbill ■ *Aceros nipalensis* 117cm

DESCRIPTION Male rich deep rufous on head, neck and underparts, black wings and tail-base, and white on distal half of tail and extreme tips of primaries. Female all black except for white tail and tips of primaries. Both sexes have corrugated ivory-coloured bill, blue skin around eye and red throat skin. **DISTRIBUTION** Bhutan across Northeast India through Myanmar to northern Indochina. North, West, East and Tenasserim, Myanmar. **HABITAT AND HABITS** Occurs in pairs or family parties in evergreen forest, usually hill slopes at 600–2,900m in mountains, but descending to lowlands for fruiting trees. Call single soft barks, repeated. **STATUS** Rare to uncommon resident.

Male   Female

Plain-pouched Hornbill ■ *Rhyticeros subruficollis* 75–90cm

DESCRIPTION Creamy-white face, neck, upper breast and tail; entirely black body and wings. Crown and hindneck dark maroon-brown. Ivory-coloured bill has ridged casque

(horn coloured, not red), and reddish, smooth (not corrugated) bill-base. Female similar but all black, with blue throat-pouch. In both sexes throat-pouch lacks dark bar. **DISTRIBUTION** Restricted to Tenasserim Peninsula, breeding in Myanmar and migrating through Thailand to northern Malaysia. **HABITAT AND HABITS** Found in tall forests in lowlands, to 915m, presumably nesting in big trees, but elsewhere known to form large flocks in non-breeding season and to make long-distance movements, to coastal forests and mangroves. **STATUS** Locally common, especially on islands in Mergui Archipelago; uncommon on mainland.

Eurasian Hoopoe
■ *Upupa epops* 28–32cm

DESCRIPTION Cinnamon-pink, with long, black-barred pink crest and butterfly-like, black and white barred wings and tail. Long, slim, downcurved bill. **DISTRIBUTION** Europe across temperate Asia, south to India and Indochina, occasionally wintering further south. Throughout Myanmar. **HABITAT AND HABITS** Found in lowlands and hills, in open country, dry, sparse woodland, villages and gardens, nesting in crevices in rocks, trees or walls, and foraging on the ground by probing with its bill for ants and grubs. **STATUS** Resident and occasional migrant.

Blue-bearded Bee-eater ■ *Nyctyornis athertoni* 33cm

DESCRIPTION Generally, plumpish green bird, with brilliant blue throat and breast giving it an appearance of a 'beard'; green back and wings, yellow lower breast, belly streaked with green, and yellow underside of tail. Bill robust, curved, almost sickle-like.
DISTRIBUTION India, along foothills of Himalaya and through Southeast Asia and southern China. North, West, East and South Myanmar. **HABITAT AND HABITS** Typically found in forest canopy or its edge, on perch that it uses to sally in pursuit of insects such as bees, wasps, termites and butterflies, and small vertebrates such as lizards. Usually solitary or in pairs, giving gruff calls. Excavates burrows in earth banks to nest. **STATUS** Uncommon resident.

Asian Green Bee-eater ■ *Merops orientalis* 20cm;
Chestnut-headed Bee-eater M. *leschenaulti* 22cm

DESCRIPTION Both have green wings and tail, and small blackish patch between throat and upper breast. Asian Green small, with rufous crown (in adult) and hindneck, and greenish breast (yellower throat and belly in juveniles). Chestnut-headed has entire crown, hindneck and back dark chestnut, richer and more extensive than in Asian Green, and yellow throat. **DISTRIBUTION** Asian Green: Iran through Indian subcontinent to mainland Southeast Asia. Chestnut-headed: similar range but more restricted to moister forests extending into Indonesia. Lowlands throughout Myanmar. **HABITAT AND HABITS** Asian Green a bird of dry country, with scattered trees and bushes, such as Central Myanmar; Chestnut-headed prefers taller forests in wetter regions. Both perch conspicuously, hawk for flying insects such as bees, wasps and dragonflies, and nest in burrows in sandy soil. **STATUS** Common residents.

Asian Green Bee-eater

Chestnut-headed Bee-eater

Blue-tailed Bee-eater ■ *Merops philippinus* 24cm

DESCRIPTION Generally light green on upperparts, wings and underparts (grading into

light blue at vent); white patch below bill; throat brownish-yellow; black eye-stripe with red iris; conspicuous bright blue tail with central streamer. **DISTRIBUTION** India and South China, through Southeast Asia and New Guinea. Breeds in North, West, East and Central Myanmar, wintering in South and Tenasserim. **HABITAT AND HABITS** Usually seen in open areas such as beach scrub, open country, plantations, gardens and rice fields. Individuals or groups often noted perched on utility lines, using them to sally from in pursuit of winged insects. Uses same perch to disarm prey such as bees of its sting. Roosts in groups. **STATUS** Common resident.

Indochinese Roller ■ *Coracias affinis* 32–34cm

DESCRIPTION Brightly coloured with azure-blue crown and wings, pale violet belly and

azure-blue vent, sandy-brown back, and lavender throat and breast. In buoyant flight shows long, broad wings with bold black (actually dark blue), and sky-blue bands and panels. **DISTRIBUTION** Northeast India across upper mainland Southeast Asia. Throughout Myanmar to 2,200m. **HABITAT AND HABITS** Occurs in open areas with scattered trees, low shrubs, and open grass and bare soil. Perches conspicuously on branches or overhead wires and drops to the ground to pick up insects. **STATUS** Common resident.

Oriental Dollarbird ■ *Eurystomus orientalis* 30cm

DESCRIPTION Heavily built, overall dark appearance with prominent red bill and feet; dark brown head; dark bluish-green body with some bluish-purple streaks on neck. White patches on wings visible in flight. **DISTRIBUTION** Resident and migrant populations from East Asia, India, Southeast Asia and Australia occur throughout Myanmar. **HABITAT AND HABITS** Commonly encountered alone or in pairs in mangroves, beach scrub, plantations and open country, usually on prominent vantage points. Often uses these perches to hunt for prey by sallying to catch winged insects such as ants and termites. Utters repeated harsh, buzzing calls. **STATUS** Uncommon resident and migrant.

Common Kingfisher ■ *Alcedo atthis* 16–18cm

DESCRIPTION One of the smallest kingfishers in the region. Bluish head, mantle and wings; back iridescent blue; ear-coverts and underparts rufous; white behind ear-coverts and chin; bill black with tinges of orange; legs red. **DISTRIBUTION** Across North Africa, Europe, temperate Asia to Southeast Asia. Throughout Myanmar. **HABITAT AND HABITS** Widespread, found across large and small waterbodies. Seen flitting across the water, giving a high-pitched *peep*, or perched low silently overlooking water in search of prey. **STATUS** Common resident and winter visitor.

Crested Kingfisher ■ *Megaceryle lugubris* 38–41cm;
Pied Kingfisher ■ *Ceryle rudis* 27–30cm

DESCRIPTION Speckled black and white kingfishers with large, all-black bills. Crested huge, with shaggy raised crest and black speckles in band across white breast; bill proportionately shorter but very robust. In flight, shows regularly banded black and white wings with rufous coverts below. Pied has neater crest, slimmer bill, and one (female) or two (male) nearly complete black bands across breast. In flight, shows black and white wings with large white panels and white lower surface. **DISTRIBUTION** Crested across foothills of Himalaya, southern China, northern Southeast Asia, through North, Central, West and East Myanmar. Pied in Africa, Middle East, South Asia, southern China and mainland Southeast Asia. **HABITAT AND HABITS** Occurs in family groups, often hovers in search of fish along large rivers and lakes to 915m (Pied) or 1,800m (Crested, which tends towards faster-flowing water and more tree-dominated landscapes). **STATUS** Uncommon residents.

Crested Kingfisher

Pied Kingfisher

Stork-billed Kingfisher ■ *Pelargopsis capensis* 37cm

DESCRIPTION Large kingfisher with massive red bill; brown head with light orange/rufous nape, throat, underparts and vent; dull bluish-green wings and tail; red feet. Bright light blue stripe down back seen in flight. **DISTRIBUTION** Resident from India to Southeast Asia, usually at low elevations. Throughout lowlands in Myanmar. **HABITAT AND HABITS** Solitary. Often spotted perched in wetlands and forested river courses. Diet mainly fish but will not hesitate to take insects and amphibians. Loud series of resonant notes in flight or when perched. **STATUS** Uncommon resident.

White-breasted Kingfisher
■ *Halcyon smyrnensis* 28cm

DESCRIPTION Brown head, sides and belly; white throat and breast resemble bib; iridescent blue back and tail; red bill and feet; black upperwing-coverts. DISTRIBUTION Widespread from Middle East, through India, China and Southeast Asia. Throughout Myanmar. HABITAT AND HABITS Found in wide range of habitats near human habitation, such as mangroves, agricultural areas, plantations, gardens and urban areas. Often seen alone on exposed perches, its calls a rapid series of descending notes. Diet varied, ranging from insects to amphibians. STATUS Common resident.

Black-capped Kingfisher ■ *Halcyon pileata* 30cm

DESCRIPTION Medium-sized kingfisher, with black head and upperwing-coverts; bright bluish mantle, upperparts and uppertail. White collar and throat grading into rufous belly (with slight scaling near throat) and vent; bright red bill and feet. DISTRIBUTION India, Myanmar, China and Korea, wintering into Southeast Asia. In Myanmar in West, Central, South and Tenasserim. HABITAT AND HABITS Usually seen singly at coastal wetlands such as mangroves, estuaries and large rivers. Less vocal than most kingfishers. STATUS Uncommon winter visitor.

Collared Kingfisher ■ *Todiramphus chloris* 25cm

DESCRIPTION Unmistakable, with bluish-green head, upperparts and wings, and white collar adjoining white underparts. Black eye-stripe inconspicuous. Bill ivory to flesh

coloured. **DISTRIBUTION** South and Southeast Asia, through New Guinea and Australia. Mostly coastal in Myanmar, in West, South and Tenasserim. **HABITAT AND HABITS** Very vocal, with initial series of 5–6 loud, harsh notes, breaking up into distinct couplets. Usually seen in mangroves, beach scrub and plantations. Varied diet ranging from small crustaceans to reptiles and amphibians inland. **STATUS** Uncommon resident.

Sooty Barbet ■ *Caloramphus hayii* 20cm

DESCRIPTION The most unbarbet-like of barbets. Plain brown above, light brown on throat, fading to near-white breast and belly. Pale-based dark bill heavy and downcurved;

feet pinkish-orange. **DISTRIBUTION** Far southern Tenasserim, Myanmar, through Peninsular Malaysia, to Sumatra. **HABITAT AND HABITS** Social, in parties of 5–10 individuals that forage in canopy but come down to head height along forested roadsides, in search of small fruits that include figs and *Macaranga*; perhaps also insects. Members of group chatter and buzz to one another, *tsee, tsee…* **STATUS** Uncommon resident.

Coppersmith Barbet ▪ *Psilopogon haemacephalus* 17cm

DESCRIPTION Smallest barbet locally. Green above and streaky buff and green below. Yellow above and below eye, and on throat; red forehead and breast-band. Sexes alike, with juveniles somewhat duller than adults. **DISTRIBUTION** Resident from Indian subcontinent through Southeast Asia to the Philippines. Throughout Myanmar below 1,500m. **HABITAT AND HABITS** Typical barbet of open country with scattered trees, parkland and even urban gardens; also plantations and mangroves. Single birds, or occasionally loose aggregations at fruiting figs, often seen perched on bare, protruding canopy twigs. Calls attention by monotonous, repeated *wink, toink, toink*, which gives it its common name. **STATUS** Common resident.

Great Barbet

▪ *Psilopogon virens* 32cm

DESCRIPTION Big, heavily built barbet, often looking blackish. Head, neck and throat very dark blue, grading into brown back, and green wings and tail; dark green-streaked yellow lower breast and flanks. Undertail-coverts red. Bill large and pale. **DISTRIBUTION** Across foothills of Himalaya into southern China and northern Southeast Asia. Hills of North, West and East Myanmar. **HABITAT AND HABITS** Found in hilly and montane evergreen forests, usually at 600–2,800m. Gives prolonged and monotonous series of single piping notes and a loud, two-note call often given in duet by other member of a pair. More often heard than seen. **STATUS** Common resident.

Blue-throated Barbet ■ *Psilopogon asiaticus* 23cm

DESCRIPTION Medium-sized barbet. Apple-green with sky-blue face and throat, black brow, and red forecrown and hindcrown separated by yellow and black band. Sexes alike

but juveniles duller than adults, especially on throat and crown. **DISTRIBUTION** Across foothills of Himalaya into southern China and northern Southeast Asia. Hills of North, West and East Myanmar. **HABITAT AND HABITS** Widespread in evergreen forests in hills and lower mountain slopes, at 400m to occasionally 2,400m. Call a repeated *took-arook, took-arook ...* . **STATUS** Common resident.

White-browed Piculet ■ *Sasia ochracea* 9cm

DESCRIPTION Tiny woodpecker with very short tail, olive-brown crown, wings and tail, and rich rufous face and underparts. Pure white streak behind eye, and forehead yellow in male, rufous in female. **DISTRIBUTION** Across foothills of Himalaya into extreme southern China and northern Southeast Asia. Hills of North, West, East and Tenasserim, Myanmar. **HABITAT AND HABITS** Found in middle and lower storeys of broadleaved evergreen forests, often in bamboo, in lowlands and hills to about 1,900m. Does not forage on trunks of big trees, but on stems of bamboo and other understorey plants, taking insects from surfaces. Often participates in mixed foraging flocks. **STATUS** Uncommon resident.

Speckled Piculet
■ *Picumnus innominatus* 10cm

DESCRIPTION Very small woodpecker with olive upperparts (greyer on upper back, greener on wings and rump), conspicuous white eyebrow and white moustache-streak; pale below with blackish speckles and bars. Male has yellowish patch on forehead, lacking in female. **DISTRIBUTION** From Himalaya, through South China and Southeast Asia, to Sumatra and Borneo. **HABITAT AND HABITS** Occurs in montane forests at about 900–1,500m, on branches and trunks of small as well as tall trees, and down to lower storey at forest edges. Usually alone or in pairs, occasionally drumming – weakly, given its size – or calling with repeated single notes, *tsik!* Found at all hill stations; sometimes caught up in mixed foraging flocks. **STATUS** Uncommon resident.

Heart-spotted Woodpecker ■ *Hemicircus canente* 16cm

DESCRIPTION Small black and white woodpecker with long crest and short tail, and white and buff wing-coverts with black, heart-shaped marks. Female has white crown, all black on male. **DISTRIBUTION** South India to Southeast Asia. In Myanmar restricted to hills of South-west, South and Tenasserim. **HABITAT AND HABITS** Uncommon in evergreen and deciduous forests to about 1,000m, in secondary forest and bamboo. Produces squeaky *ki-yew* and high-pitched *kee, kee, kee, kee*, and very weak drumming. **STATUS** Uncommon resident.

Rufous Woodpecker ■ *Micropternus brachyurus* 25cm

DESCRIPTION Plumage overall rufous-brown, slightly darker on head and tail, with black bars on back, wings and tail. No significant crest. Male has patch of red below eye,

absent in female, but not very conspicuous against generally brown colour. **DISTRIBUTION** Himalayan foothills, eastern India and Sri Lanka, through southern China to Hainan, south to Borneo and Java. Throughout lowlands in Myanmar. **HABITAT AND HABITS** Found in lowland forests, from sea level to about 1,000m, where it may just enter lower montane forests; and down into mangroves and tall secondary forests. Usually in tree crowns, coming lower at forest edges and in clearings. Specializes in eating ants. **STATUS** Uncommon resident.

Buff-rumped Woodpecker ■ *Meiglyptes grammithorax* 17cm

DESCRIPTION Small woodpecker, finely barred black and white all over head and underparts; more widely striped on back, and still more widely on wings and tail. Male has small scarlet moustache-streak, absent in female. **DISTRIBUTION** Southern Tenasserim, Myanmar, to Peninsular Malaysia, Sumatra and Borneo. **HABITAT AND HABITS** Occurs in middle storey of mixed evergreen forest, tall secondary woodland and forest edges, in lowlands to 760m. Drums briefly and softly, and gives trilling call as well as single notes. **STATUS** Uncommon resident.

Greater Yellownape ■ *Chrysophlegma flavinucha* 33cm

DESCRIPTION Adult dull olive-green above, lighter greenish-grey below. Triangular crest tipped bright yellow, in line running down nape and neck; primaries banded black and brown. Male has yellow throat, female inconspicuous light rufous. **DISTRIBUTION** Himalaya discontinuously through southern China and Southeast Asia to Sumatra. Widespread in hills of Myanmar. **HABITAT AND HABITS** Fairly common in montane forest at about 300–1,500m. In middle storey, often near quiet roadsides. Call a spaced *chup; chup; chrr*; also single soft screech, *kwee*, which may be repeated in whittering series. Only occasionally drums. **STATUS** Uncommon resident.

Black-headed Woodpecker ■ *Picus erythropygius* 33cm

DESCRIPTION Very handsome, medium-sized woodpecker. Black face and hindneck sharply contrast with bright yellow throat and neck-sides, yellow fading gradually down breast to faintly barred flanks. Above, wings green, with banded dark and light primaries showing in flight, as does red rump. Male has red crown-patch, lacking in female. **DISTRIBUTION** Central, South, East and Tenasserim, Myanmar, through Northern Thailand to Indochina. **HABITAT AND HABITS** Occurs in dry forests in lowlands to about 1,000m, including in stands of broadleaved and coniferous trees. **STATUS** Rare resident.

Great Slaty Woodpecker ■ *Mulleripicus pulverulentus* 45–51cm

DESCRIPTION Very big, rather gawky, grey woodpecker, a little paler on head and neck, darker on wings and tail. Throat light buff; male has prominent red moustache-streak, absent in female.

DISTRIBUTION Himalaya to mainland Southeast Asia, Java and Borneo. Extensive lowland forests in North, East and Tenasserim, Myanmar. HABITAT AND HABITS Found in tall forests in lowlands, occasionally to about 1,050m, foraging quite high up on trunks and boughs of big trees in deciduous and semi-evergreen forests. Feeds largely on ants and grubs below bark. Small, laughing flocks as the birds follow one another from tree to tree. STATUS Uncommon resident.

Rufous-bellied Woodpecker
■ *Dendrocopos hyperythrus* 17–23cm

DESCRIPTION Very distinctive, with white face-patch around eye. Rest of face, neck and underparts rufous; back, wings and tail banded broadly in black and white. Male has scarlet crown, spotted black and white in female. DISTRIBUTION Patchy from Himalaya to Indochina. North, West and East Myanmar; regularly seen in Natmataung National Park, Chin State. HABITAT AND HABITS Occurs in hilly and montane areas at about 600–3,000m, in deciduous and evergreen, mixed broadleaved and coniferous forests. STATUS Uncommon resident.

Fulvous-breasted Woodpecker
■ *Dendrocopos macei* 18–21cm

DESCRIPTION Buff face, breast and belly, with light barring on flanks and red vent; back and wings chequered black and white; black moustache-stripe petering out into narrow streaks on upper breast. Crown scarlet in male, black in female. **DISTRIBUTION** Himalaya through Northeast India, to North and West Myanmar. **HABITAT AND HABITS** Found in lowlands and hills to about 1,200m, in deciduous forests, secondary woodland and overgrown cultivation. **STATUS** Uncommon resident.

Collared Falconet ■ *Microhierax caerulescens* 16.5cm;
Black-thighed Falconet ■ *M. fringillarius* 16cm

DESCRIPTION Tiny raptors, black above and white below. Black-thighed has narrow white line behind eye curling around black cheek-patch; narrow white forehead, throat, breast and marks on tail. Collared has wider white brow and forehead, and white forms neck-collar. Belly and vent rufous, and in juveniles rufous tinge to pale band from cheek to brow. **DISTRIBUTION** Foothills of Himalaya and most of lowland mainland Southeast Asia. Black-thighed only in far South, Myanmar. **HABITAT AND HABITS** Sociable, in loose family associations in canopy of forests, northern deciduous and mixed evergreen (Collared), or Sundaic evergreen (Black-thighed), on exposed perches. Feed on large insects (katydids, locusts, cicadas and butterflies), and occasionally small birds and mammals. **STATUS** Uncommon residents.

Collared Falconet

Black-thighed Falconet

Common Kestrel ■ *Falco tinnunculus* 28–35cm

DESCRIPTION Male has bright rufous wings and back, spotted with black, grey head with indistinct dark moustache-streak, and grey tail with white tip and black subterminal

band; buff spotted with black below. Female light brown on back, wings and tail; tail barred; wings densely spotted; head and underparts more heavily marked than in male. **DISTRIBUTION** Across Palaearctic from Europe and North Africa to East Asia, migrating south in non-breeding season. Found throughout in winter months. **HABITAT AND HABITS** Occurs in open country with scattered trees, seeking prey while perched on wires or exposed branches, or by hovering over rice fields and grassland. **STATUS** Common winter visitor.

Laggar Falcon ■ *Falco jugger* 41–46cm;
Peregrine Falcon ■ *F. peregrinus* 40–48cm

DESCRIPTION Large, dark falcons; upperparts and tail dark grey; throat and underparts cream with dark streaks and heavy barring. Laggar has streaked brown crown, whiter breast than Peregrine, and blackish flank-patch, narrow moustache and unbarred tail. Peregrine has dark hood interrupted by pale cheeks separating broad dark moustache from rear part of head and neck. Narrow orbital ring and yellow legs; bill yellow at base and dark towards tip. **DISTRIBUTION** Laggar in South Asia including Myanmar dry zone, breeding

Laggar Falcon

on temples in Bagan. Peregrine nearly global with non-breeding migrants and localized residents throughout Myanmar. **HABITAT AND HABITS** Peregrine found almost anywhere, from coastal wetlands to migrants over forest; Laggar in drier open country. **STATUS** Localized resident (Laggar); rare resident with uncommon winter visitors (Peregrine).

Laggar Falcon

Peregrine Falcon

Vernal Hanging-parrot ▪ *Loriculus vernalis* 14cm

DESCRIPTION Tiny, short-tailed, grass-green parrot, with red bill, orange legs and dark red rump. Male has sky-blue area on throat and upper breast (less pronounced in female); both sexes reveal bluish lower surface of wing in flight. DISTRIBUTION South and Southeast Asia. Throughout Myanmar. HABITAT AND HABITS Lowlands to about 1,500m in evergreen, semi-evergreen and deciduous forests, usually in canopy of forest but lower at edges and in cultivation. Feeds on nectar and soft fruits. Small size makes it difficult to find in tree canopies; more often heard or seen in flight. STATUS Locally common resident around blooming and fruiting trees.

Grey-headed Parakeet ▪ *Psittacula finschii* 36–40cm;
Red-breasted Parakeet ▪ *P. alexandri* 33–37cm

DESCRIPTION Green with grey head. Bill has red upper and black lower mandible, and tail has blue base. More lilac head in female than in male, and juveniles have green head and all-yellow bill. Red-breasted bigger, with heavy black stripe separating light grey head from deep pink breast. Bill with red upper and black lower mandible in male, all-black in female. DISTRIBUTION North-east Himalaya foothills through mainland Southeast Asia; Red-breasted has similar range extending further west along Himalaya foothills and south into Indonesia. HABITAT AND HABITS Occur in lowlands to 1,200m, in broadleaved evergreen and deciduous forests, and adjacent cultivation, in small parties, forming large flocks when food supply is abundant. STATUS Locally common residents. Threatened due to harvesting from the wild for pet trade.

Grey-headed Parakeet

Red-breasted Parakeet

Alexandrine Parakeet ■ *Psittacula eupatria* 50–58cm;
Rose-ringed Parakeet ■ *P. krameri* 40–42cm

DESCRIPTION Alexandrine notably large, with heavy, entirely red bill and dark red shoulder-patch; male has narrow ring of black from throat, becoming pink around back of neck (lacking in female). Rose-ringed smaller and with narrower neck ring (lacking in female), and no red shoulder-patch; bill red above with black lower mandible.
DISTRIBUTION Alexandrine across South and Southeast Asia; Rose-ringed across tropical Africa, South Asia, and Central and South Myanmar. **HABITAT AND HABITS** Mostly in deciduous forests in lowlands to 915m; Rose-ringed also in cultivation and villages. **STATUS** Uncommon residents. Both harvested from the wild and sold as pets.

Alexandrine Parakeet

Rose-ringed Parakeet

Gurney's Pitta
■ *Hydrornis gurneyi* 18–20cm ⓔ

DESCRIPTION Male has blue crown, black mask, yellow throat contrasting with black underparts, and flanks heavily barred black and yellow; brown wings. Female similarly patterned, but rufous crown, dark mask, white throat and entire underparts buffy-white barred with black. **DISTRIBUTION** Endemic to small region in south Tenasserim. Formerly in adjacent Thailand where now functionally extinct. **HABITAT AND HABITS** Occurs in extreme lowlands, below 160m, in forests and adjacent tree plantations. **STATUS** Very rare and declining resident in extremely restricted range because of expanding clearance of forest for agriculture and land speculation.

Blue-winged Pitta ▪ *Pitta moluccensis* 26cm

DESCRIPTION Brilliantly particoloured with black mask, buff underparts with red beneath tail, green upperparts and bright blue wings. In flight, wings bold blue and black with white panels, like those of many other pittas and some kingfishers. Very similar but big-billed **Mangrove Pitta** P. *megarhyncha* occurs along mangrove coasts. **DISTRIBUTION** Wet-season breeding visitor in mainland Southeast Asia, including East, South and Tenasserim Myanmar, migrating south to Peninsular Malaysia, Sumatra and Borneo. **HABITAT AND HABITS** Usually alone, in lowland forest or dense vegetation in plantations or even large gardens, where it hops on the ground, turning leaf litter to seek insects and grubs. Migrates at night; many records of birds stunned by hitting buildings when disorientated by lights. Call a four-note *chew-chew; chew-chew*, heard extensively each May and June. **STATUS** Locally common breeding visitor.

Long-tailed Broadbill
▪ *Psarisomus dalhousiae* 26cm

DESCRIPTION Like a parakeet, brilliant grass-green bill and wings, paler turquoise on breast, bluer on primaries and long tail. Narrow white collar (perhaps better defined in female than in male) joins yellow throat, with yellow patch over ear; sides and top of head black, with small blue skull-cap. **DISTRIBUTION** Resident from central Himalayan foothills through to Borneo. **HABITAT AND HABITS** Inhabits montane and hill forests to about 1,500m and down to about 850m, with scattered records as low as 250m in northern foothills. Occurs in small parties seeking insects on foliage and twigs of trees in middle and upper storeys; occasionally in small trees along quiet forest roads. Flock members bob tails and call to each other in descending series of trills. **STATUS** Uncommon resident.

Silver-breasted Broadbill ■ *Serilophus lunatus* 16cm

DESCRIPTION Most elegant, with silvery-grey head and breast (crossed in female by silver-white line), shading to ashy-brown back and rich chestnut rump. Conspicuous black eyebrow, and wings black with flashes of blue and white. Bill silvery-blue and yellow. **DISTRIBUTION** East and Tenasserim, Myanmar, and southern China, across Indochina to Sumatra. **HABITAT AND HABITS** Occurs to about 1,200m and down to variable altitude, sometimes as low as 230m, in middle and lower storeys. Perhaps a hill-slope rather than strictly montane bird. Nest hung from small tree over hillside gully; lining replenished with fresh green leaves throughout incubation, as in other broadbills. Thought to feed on insects. **STATUS** Uncommon resident.

Female

Male

Green Broadbill ■ *Calyptomena viridis* 16cm

DESCRIPTION Entirely brilliant glowing green. More emerald in male with yellow spot before eye, black spot behind ear, three black wing-bars and more bluish undertail-coverts

and tail. Female more grass-green, lacking markings but with same blue beneath tail. **DISTRIBUTION** Resident from about 16°N in Myanmar, south through Thailand and Malaysia, to Borneo. **HABITAT AND HABITS** Occurs in lowland evergreen rainforests from sea level to about 760m, with occasional long-distance dispersal possible at other altitudes. In pairs, singly or in small groups, snatching fruits and some insects in flight. Nest a neat hanging bag suspended from an understorey twig, sometimes at human head height. Call an accelerating, descending series of taps; also short, cat-like moans and frog-like croaks. **STATUS** Uncommon resident.

Maroon Oriole ■ *Oriolus traillii* 24–28cm

DESCRIPTION Male entirely deep maroon-red, but for black head and wings. Female similar but duller, with entire underside from chin to belly white with narrow dark streaks, and undertail-coverts and tail reddish. Bill and eye grey-white. **DISTRIBUTION** Himalaya to Southeast Asia and southern China. North, West, Central, East and northern Tenasserim, Myanmar, with some local movements in winter. **HABITAT AND HABITS** Hilly and montane land usually at 450–2,700m, in middle storey and canopy of mostly evergreen broadleaved forests. Utters varied musical whistles. **STATUS** Common resident.

Black-hooded Oriole ■ *Oriolus xanthornus* 23cm;
Black-naped Oriole ■ *O. chinensis* 26cm

DESCRIPTION Black-hooded adult brilliant yellow, with black head and upper breast, black tail and wings with yellow markings. Young birds duller, streaked with whitish on throat. Male Black-naped brilliant yellow over most of plumage; even black wings and tail have yellow bars and flashes; black band from bill through eye, joining at back of head. Females slightly duller, more olive above; juveniles olive-green, streaky below. **DISTRIBUTION** Black-hooded resident in South and mainland Southeast Asia. Black-naped breeds in East Asia and northern Southeast Asia, and migrates to Myanmar and much of Southeast Asia in winter. West and Central Myanmar year round. **HABITAT AND HABITS** Black-hooded a bird of forest and edges in rural areas; Black-naped also in gardens, parkland, orchards and secondary woodland in lowlands, foraging for all sorts of fruits and insects; also mangroves. Much interaction between individuals, particularly the loud fluting calls of Black-naped, *ku-eyou-ou*, with chasing, following and displacement from food sources. **STATUS** Common resident (Black-hooded); common migrant and winter visitor (Black-naped).

Black-hooded Oriole

Black-naped Oriole

Slender-billed Oriole
■ *Oriolus tenuirostris* 23–26cm

DESCRIPTION Very like female Black-naped Oriole (p. 83), but black band through eye and around nape narrower, and pink bill slightly longer and narrower. **DISTRIBUTION** Himalaya foothills, through North, West, Central and East Myanmar, to north and central Indochina. **HABITAT AND HABITS** Typically occurs at about 600–1900m; more usual above 1,000m, but greatly overlaps with Black-naped in evergreen broadleaved and sometimes coniferous forests. Whistled song delivered more rapidly. **STATUS** Uncommon resident.

Black-headed Shrike-babbler ■ *Pteruthius rufiventer* 21cm;
Blyth's Shrike-babbler ■ *P. aeralatus* 17cm

DESCRIPTION Black-headed larger, with pale grey throat grading into buff belly; sharply contrasting with black head, brown back and rump, black wings and tail. Blyth's pearly-white below; crown and mask of male black with white eyebrow, and back grey-black; black wings and tail, with golden inner secondaries. Females similar respectively, but head pattern and body colours all subdued. **DISTRIBUTION** Black-headed in Eastern Himalayan and associated ridges in North and West Myanmar; Blyth's more widely distributed across southern China and through ridges of Southeast Asia. North, West, East and Tenasserim, Myanmar. **HABITAT AND HABITS** Found in hill and montane forests, mainly in canopy but also at forest edges. Insectivorous, taking caterpillars and other invertebrates. **STATUS** Rare (Black-headed); common resident (Blyth's).

Black-headed Shrike-babbler   *Blyth's Shrike-babbler*

Green Shrike-babbler
■ *Pteruthius xanthochlorus* 12cm

DESCRIPTION Small and rather nondescript, with white throat grading to pale yellow belly; dark grey head sharply defined against white throat, and grey-brown wings, back and tail. Narrow pale ring around eye; short, thick bill. Female similar to male but colours more subdued. **DISTRIBUTION** Himalaya, across North and West Myanmar, into Southwest China. Often seen in Natmataung National Park. **HABITAT AND HABITS** Seen singly or in pairs, often in mixed foraging flocks, in montane forests at about 1,700–2,800m. **STATUS** Uncommon resident.

Jerdon's Minivet ■ *Pericrocotus albifrons* 15–16cm

DESCRIPTION Pied minivet, with black (male) or grey (female) crown, back, wings and tail; white forehead and eye-stripe, white wing-bars, and white below with orange-buff to buffy-grey upper breast-patch. In flight, rump shows orange centre. **DISTRIBUTION** Endemic to forests of Central Myanmar; regularly seen around temples in Bagan. **HABITAT AND HABITS** Occurs in pairs, family parties or small flocks, in dry forest and thorn scrub, foraging in crowns of scattered trees. **STATUS** Uncommon resident.

Long-tailed Minivet ■ *Pericrocotus ethologus* 18–20cm;
Scarlet Minivet ■ *P. flammeus* 19–21cm

DESCRIPTION Both brilliant red and black, but Long-tailed slightly smaller, slimmer, with longer tail showing red only on outermost feathers; male Scarlet has more red in shorter tail, and separate red mark on tertiaries. Females and young males grey above and yellow below, Long-tailed with single yellow wing-panel; Scarlet shows several smaller but separate yellow wing-panels on primaries, secondaries and tertiaries. **DISTRIBUTION** Long-tailed from Afghanistan, to southern China and Indochina; Scarlet from Himalaya, to Greater Sundas and the Philippines. **HABITAT AND HABITS** Like other minivets, prefer crowns of tall trees, in lowland and hill forests – Long-tailed at 450–3,100m, Scarlet from lowlands to 1,700m, especially evergreen forest. Take all sorts of small invertebrates. After breeding during first half of year, pairs group into small flocks. **STATUS** Common residents.

Long-tailed Minivet   *Scarlet Minivet*   *Scarlet Minivet*

Black-winged Cuckooshrike
■ *Lalage melaschistos* 22–25cm

DESCRIPTION Medium-grey with darker head and blackish wings and tail. Female paler overall than male, with paler vent and whitish tips to tail feathers visible from below and in flight. Other cuckooshrike species in region bigger and paler. **DISTRIBUTION** From foothills of Himalaya, across East and Central China and south through mainland Southeast Asia, travelling further south during winter. **HABITAT AND HABITS** Found in evergreen forests at 300–1,900m, and occasionally in more open habitats and lower elevations on migration or post-breeding dispersal. **STATUS** Uncommon resident with some wider movement in winter.

Ashy Woodswallow
■ *Artamus fuscus* 16–18cm

DESCRIPTION Stocky, smooth-plumaged, grey-brown bird with rather long wings (reaching tip of tail when perched). Slightly paler buffy-grey below, and robust pale bill with darker tip. Juveniles a little duller and paler than adults. **DISTRIBUTION** Across South and Southeast Asia. **HABITAT AND HABITS** Seen on wires and bare tree crowns, hawking for insects, often flying in long glides on triangular, starling-like wings. Social and argumentative, roosting in small groups lined up along the same branch. **STATUS** Common resident.

Bar-winged Flycatcher-shrike ■ *Hemipus picatus* 15cm

DESCRIPTION Black cap and mask, bordered with white below; smoky-grey breast and belly; black wings and tail, with long, clear white wing-bar from carpals across coverts to tips of secondaries. Female browner above and paler below than male, and in juveniles wing-bar is buff. **DISTRIBUTION** South and Southeast Asia, to Malay Peninsula, Sumatra and Borneo. **HABITAT AND HABITS** Occurs in hill and montane forests from 500m upwards, sometimes in rubber and other plantations. Often moves through middle storey with other birds in mixed foraging flocks, or in pairs. **STATUS** Uncommon resident.

Common Iora ■ *Aegithina tiphia* 13cm

DESCRIPTION Green above with black tail and black or green in male on crown; yellow below, fading to white on undertail-coverts that curl sideways and up over rump to make

rump seem white; wings black with two white bars and pale fringes. **DISTRIBUTION** Resident from South and Southeast Asia, to Greater Sundas and the Philippines. **HABITAT AND HABITS** Takes insects from foliage in plantations, trees in parks, mangroves and roadsides, and entering edges of lowland evergreen forests. Often forages high in canopy, for example in tall *Albizia* trees, but also comes down to understorey. In display flight from tree to tree, male displays false white rump, while singing; huge range of calls and song types. **STATUS** Common resident.

White-throated Fantail ■ *Rhipidura albicollis* 19cm

DESCRIPTION Blackish above and below, except for white throat-triangle, white brow and white tips to tail feathers. Juveniles duller and browner, with brow and throat-mark less well defined than in

adults. **DISTRIBUTION** Resident from western Himalaya to Borneo. **HABITAT AND HABITS** Occurs in a variety of woodland, in middle and lower storeys. Seeks insects and is one of the most common birds, with a repeated tuneful song of 7–8 notes. Common in mixed foraging flocks. Nest a cup slung in fork of small lateral branch in middle storey; it is hardly big enough to contain two growing young. **STATUS** Common resident.

Black Drongo ▪ *Dicrurus macrocercus* 28cm;
Ashy Drongo ▪ *D. leucophaeus* 26–28cm

DESCRIPTION Black of open farmland and rice fields with cattle, glossy black all over, with upswept, fish-tail tail-tip. Ashy has less upswept tail, and some populations may have paler sides of face and ruby-red eyes. **DISTRIBUTION** Black from Iran to southern China and Indochina. Ashy from Afghanistan to southern China, the Philippines and Lesser Sundas. **HABITAT AND HABITS** Predominantly occurs in agricultural land, with Ashy also in forest edges and mangroves, and open ground with fairly close spacing of trees, providing points for foraging on insects; migrants tend to occur more in parkland and gardens. Both species able to mimic calls of other birds. **STATUS** Common resident, supplemented by greater numbers moving during migration (Black); common forest resident, with paler races visiting in winter (Ashy).

Black Drongo

Ashy Drongo

Bronzed Drongo ▪ *Dicrurus aeneus* 24cm;
Greater Racquet-tailed Drongo ▪ *D. paradiseus* 32–57cm

DESCRIPTION Noisy, conspicuous glossy black birds with red eyes. Greater Racquet-tailed has two outer-tail feathers projecting as bare 'wires', with one rounded and twisted racquet each side. One or both racquets may be missing due to moult or damage, then closely resembling Bronzed, which is smaller, with outer-tail feathers very slightly upturned. **DISTRIBUTION** Across South and Southeast Asia, to Borneo (both). **HABITAT AND HABITS** Occur in canopy and middle storey of lowland and hill forests, and in mangroves, tree plantations (rubber and oil palm), parkland with abundant trees, and secondary woodland. Fly out to catch passing insects from high perches. Typically in pairs and utter wide range of calls, Greater Racquet-tailed giving good imitations of many other birds. **STATUS** Uncommon residents.

Bronzed Drongo

Greater Racquet-tailed Drongo

Black-naped Monarch ■ *Hypothymis azurea* 16cm

DESCRIPTION Bright blue forequarters shading down to ashy-brown wings and tail, and whitish belly. Male has black throat-bar, crown-spot and dab over bill; female has greyer

breast and black dab over bill. **DISTRIBUTION** Resident from India to the Philippines and Lesser Sundas. **HABITAT AND HABITS** Occurs in lower and middle storeys of lowland and hill forests. Usually alone or in pairs, or in mixed foraging flocks. One of the common birds glimpsed during trips along forested rivers, aerial flycatching in forests and occasionally bathing by diving into the water. **STATUS** Common resident.

Oriental Paradise-flycatcher ■ *Terpsiphone affinis* 22–40cm

DESCRIPTION Female has black hood shading down to grey neck and breast, to whitish belly; rufous-chestnut wings and tail. Male either similar with very long tail (nearly triple body length); or body, wings and tail pure white with fine black edgings to some feathers. **DISTRIBUTION** Resident from Northeast India across Southeast Asia and Indonesia. **HABITAT AND HABITS** Male spectacular and not rare; resident in middle and upper storeys of tall lowland forests and secondary woodland. Insectivorous, taking fairly big insects, and usually solitary. **STATUS** Uncommon resident, previously lumped with **Indian Paradise-flycatcher** *T. paradisi* in Central and South Asia and **Chinese Paradise-flycatcher** *T. incei* breeding in north-east Asia, wintering to Southeast Asia.

Female   *Male*

Crested Shrikejay
■ *Platylophus galericulatus* 32cm

DESCRIPTION Blackish head and body with fine vertical or forwards-tilting crest; white marks around eye and white patch on neck-sides. **DISTRIBUTION** Southernmost Myanmar, to Sumatra, Borneo and Java. **HABITAT AND HABITS** Not easy to see, but can be curious, raising a shrike-like rattling chatter when it sees people. Keeps to middle and lower storeys of forests. Usually solitary or in pairs, seeking invertebrates like beetles, grasshoppers, wasps and cicadas. **STATUS** Uncommon resident in far south Tenasserim. Threatened due to forest loss.

Brown Shrike ■ *Lanius cristatus* 19–20cm

DESCRIPTION Several subspecies differ in tone, but always have plain back, never finely barred. Black mask, pale supercilium and brown or grey crown; back and tail brown, undersides off white; bill relatively small. Sexes alike.

DISTRIBUTION Resident in vast areas of temperate East Asia, from 70°E south through China. Migrates throughout Myanmar as far as the Philippines, Java and Lesser Sundas. **HABITAT AND HABITS** Occurs in cultivation, gardens, open ground with bushes, scattered trees and grassland, advertising territory with chattering calls. Seen singly, on fences, trees and bush tops, descending to catch invertebrates on the ground, mostly beetles and grasshoppers, but occasionally lizards and small birds. **STATUS** Common winter visitor.

Burmese Shrike ■ *Lanius colluroides* 19–21cm

DESCRIPTION Rather clean, bright-looking shrike with dark grey crown, black mask contrasting with pure white underparts, and rufous mantle and rump. As in other shrikes, juveniles have more subdued colours and scaly markings over crown, back and underparts. **DISTRIBUTION** Throughout northern and central Southeast Asia. **HABITAT AND HABITS** Resident in forest clearings and edges to 2,000m, spreading further south into lowlands and cultivation outside breeding season. **STATUS** Uncommon resident.

Female

Male

Long-tailed Shrike ■ *Lanius schach* 25–28cm;
Grey-backed Shrike ■ *L. tephronotus* 22–25cm

DESCRIPTION Black face, crown and nape sharply cut off from light rufous back distinguish Long-tailed from smaller Grey-backed, which has shorter tail, light grey crown and back, and lacks white patch at bases of primaries. In both, peach-buff flanks differ from clean white of the Burmese Shrike (above). **DISTRIBUTION** Resident from Central Asia to New Guinea, and throughout Myanmar. From Himalaya, to India and across much of China, wintering in North, Central, West, East and South Myanmar. **HABITAT AND HABITS** Both can occur in open rice fields and grassland with shrubs, across broad altitude range. Perch prominently and take mainly insects. **STATUS** Common resident (Long-tailed); common winter visitor (Grey-backed).

Long-tailed Shrike   Grey-backed Shrike

Hooded Treepie
■ *Crypsirina cucullata* 31cm

DESCRIPTION Pale grey body and wings, with black head, neck and flight feathers, and long, spatulate tail (up to two-thirds of total length), in which central feathers black, outer feathers pale. Young birds have grey rather than black head. **DISTRIBUTION** Endemic to Myanmar dry zone across plains of Ayeyarwady and Sittang Rivers in North, Central and South. **HABITAT AND HABITS** Occurs in lowlands to 950m, in dry deciduous forests and scattered trees in open country, and cultivation. Seen in pairs or small groups. Birds give whirring calls to keep in touch with each another. **STATUS** Uncommon resident. Threatened due to habitat loss.

Grey Treepie
■ *Dendrocitta formosae* 36–40cm

DESCRIPTION Relatively substantially built treepie with blackish face-mask or hood sharply cut off from grey hindcrown; body largely grey but shading into fawn face, breast, brown scapulars and black wings with white spot on bases of primaries; rufous vent, and long, grey and black tail. **DISTRIBUTION** Across foothills of Himalaya into southern China and northern Southeast Asia, especially North, West and East Myanmar. **HABITAT AND HABITS** Occurs at about 450–2,250m, in broadleaved evergreen forests and forest edges. Small flocks venture out to isolated trees, noisily calling with medley of buzzing, chattering and bell-like notes. **STATUS** Common resident.

Collared Treepie
■ *Dendrocitta frontalis* 36–38cm

DESCRIPTION Slimmer and more brightly coloured than the Grey Treepie (p. 93). Black hood sharply defined all around; back and entire belly bright rufous; wing-coverts show as broad, ash-grey panel sandwiched between rufous back and dark wings. **DISTRIBUTION** Northeast India, northern Myanmar and Southwest China, with separate population in north Vietnam. **HABITAT AND HABITS** Found in broadleaved forests in hills to 1,220m, disturbed forests and bamboo, and abandoned cultivation. Occurs in small, noisy parties like other treepies, though quality of calls differs. **STATUS** Near-endemic in North Myanmar.

Yellow-billed Blue Magpie ■ *Urocissa flavirostris* 55–66cm;
Red-billed Blue Magpie ■ *U. erythroryncha* 53–68cm

DESCRIPTION Very long-tailed, with azure-blue wings; secondaries and tail feathers tipped black and white. Slightly smaller Yellow-billed has greyer wings and back, yellow bill and pale spot on nape. Red-billed has brighter, bluer wings and tail, red bill and clear white patch from crown to back. **DISTRIBUTION** Yellow-billed across Himalaya into North and West Myanmar. Red-billed more widespread across North, West, Central, East and northern Tenasserim, Myanmar, into northern Southeast Asia and eastern China. **HABITAT AND HABITS** Found in broadleaved evergreen and pine forests, forest edges and secondary regrowth; Yellow-billed in hills at 1,220–3,100m, Red-billed below 1,950m. Occur in small parties in middle storey; conspicuous in flight. **STATUS** Locally common residents.

Yellow-billed Blue Magpie   *Red-billed Blue Magpie*

Common Green Magpie ▪ *Cissa chinensis* 37–39cm

DESCRIPTION Brilliant pale lime-green all over, with yellow tinge on crown; tips of inner wing feathers have black and white marks; long tail with black and white tips. Bill, legs and skin around eye brilliant red. **DISTRIBUTION** From Himalayan foothills throughout Myanmar to northern Indochina, Peninsular Malaysia, Sumatra and Borneo. **HABITAT AND HABITS** Found in hill and montane forests. Often silent and inconspicuous, then suddenly becomes active and vocal. Range of whistles and buzzing notes may reveal one or a small group in dense vegetation of middle or lower storey, seeking beetles, caterpillars, snails and other invertebrates. **STATUS** Uncommon resident.

House Crow ▪ *Corvus splendens* 42cm;
Large-billed Crow ▪ *C. macrorhynchos* 47–50cm

DESCRIPTION House glossy black all over, with paler zone of grey over hind-face and neck down to breast-sides. Colour develops with age, juveniles looking entirely black. Large-billed considerably bulkier, with much bigger, arched bill, and entirely glossy black. **DISTRIBUTION** Naturally resident in Myanmar; Afghanistan, through India and southern China to south-west Thailand. Widely introduced by humans elsewhere, as far as South Africa, Europe, North America and Australia. Large-billed ranges from India across Southeast and Northeast Asia. Both throughout Myanmar. **HABITAT AND HABITS** House typical of towns, forming noisy communal roosts and mainly dependent on human refuse. Large-billed tends to occur in rural areas as well, including farmland and villages. **STATUS** Common residents.

House Crow

Large-billed Crow

Large-billed Crow

Sultan Tit ■ *Melanochlora sultanea* 20–21cm

DESCRIPTION Heavily built, strong-billed tit. Male has black head, upper breast, wings and tail; striking erect, shaggy yellow crest; yellow lower breast, belly and undertail-coverts. Female similar, but areas that are black in male (face, wings and upper breast) are brownish-black to olive brown. **DISTRIBUTION** Himalaya to Peninsular Malaysia. Throughout most of Myanmar. **HABITAT AND HABITS** Known from range of forest types, including lowland and hill forests, to about 1,200m in lower montane forest. Best glimpsed from roadsides or tracks giving views into upper storey. Call an attractive repeated, modulated whistle. **STATUS** Uncommon resident.

Green-backed Tit ■ *Parus monticolus* 12–14cm;
Yellow-cheeked Tit ■ *Machlolophus spilonotus* 13–15cm

DESCRIPTION Green-backed crestless, with large white cheek-patch; head otherwise black. Back plain green, and black band down centre of breast from throat to belly. Yellow-cheeked crested, with yellow brow, cheek and nape-patch, black line through eye, narrower black line down centre of breast, mottled green back and broader white wing-bars. **DISTRIBUTION** Green-backed across Himalaya into North and West Myanmar, and up into Southwest and Central China. Yellow-cheeked more restricted to north-east Himalaya and across Myanmar, including East, and into southern China and higher elevations of Indochina. **HABITAT AND HABITS** Both occur in broadleaved evergreen forests at about 800–2,700m; Green-backed in wider variety of forest types, including pine, foraging often in small parties or mixed flocks. **STATUS** Common resident (Green-backed); uncommon resident (Yellow-cheeked).

Green-backed Tit   *Yellow-cheeked Tit*

Burmese Bushlark ■ *Mirafra microptera* 14–15cm e

DESCRIPTION Mostly subdued brown, streaky dark feather centres on buff plumage, browner on back and especially on crown, with pale eye-stripe; like other bushlarks has rich rufous panel in primaries. Bold black spots in zone across upper breast. **DISTRIBUTION** Restricted to dry zone in North and Central Myanmar. **HABITAT AND HABITS** Occurs in dry country and scrub with scattered trees, from lowlands to about 1,300m. Forages on the ground and flies up to trees or wires when disturbed. **STATUS** Endemic, common resident.

Sand Lark ■ *Alaudala raytal* 14cm

DESCRIPTION Small, washed out lark, very pale mottled sandy-grey above with whiter underparts, and zone of inconspicuous streaks on upper breast; short tail and relatively slim bill. **DISTRIBUTION** Iran through northern Indian subcontinent, and along Ayeyarwady River in South and Central Myanmar. **HABITAT AND HABITS** Found in lowlands, often foraging on bare, sandy ground or dry ground with sparse grasses, usually near rivers or dunes, or occasionally in cultivation. **STATUS** Locally common resident.

Zitting Cisticola ■ *Cisticola juncidis* 10–14cm;
Golden-headed Cisticola ■ *C. exilis* 9–11cm

DESCRIPTION Very small warblers, rufous-brown boldly streaked with black above, and light buff below. Zitting has whitish eye-stripe, streaks on back extending to rear neck, and rufous-tinged rump. Golden-headed has buffy eye-stripe, plain rear neck, rump a little less bright, and whitish tail-tips duller and less clear. Breeding male Golden-headed has unstreaked golden-buff head and neck, including crown. **DISTRIBUTION** Zitting across Old World. Golden-headed limited to South and Southeast Asia, through Indonesia to Australia. **HABITAT AND HABITS** Found in wet-growing rice and stubble, wet grassland and scrub, or (Golden-headed) in drier habitat. Hard to see but makes long, wavering song flight (Zitting), or short song flight as well as singing from perch (Golden-headed). **STATUS** Common residents.

Zitting Cisticola   *Golden-headed Cisticola*

Burmese Prinia
■ *Prinia cooki* 15–18cm

DESCRIPTION Dull, streaky-brown with long, graduated tail; darker than other prinias in region, with streaks on back rather obscure, whitish-buff underparts not or hardly streaked, and poorly defined pale eye-stripe. Bill black in breeding male, pale in female and in non-breeding season. Previously included in **Brown Prinia** *P. polychroa*. **DISTRIBUTION** Found from South and Central across East Myanmar to southern China. **HABITAT AND HABITS** Lowlands to 800m, in dry grassland in forest edges and undergrowth in dry dipterocarp forest, sometimes emerging from dense tangle to sing from top of bush. **STATUS** Uncommon resident. Data Deficient due to recent taxonomic changes.

Grey-breasted Prinia
■ *Prinia hodgsoni* 10–12cm

DESCRIPTION Small, short-tailed, rufous-backed prinia, hard to distinguish from **Rufescent Prinia** *P. rufescens*, but on average less buff below with slightly more slender bill, and white throat with slightly sharper cut-off from grey sides of face; slight supercilium restricted to area above and in front of eye. **DISTRIBUTION** Throughout South and Southeast Asia, including most of Myanmar. **HABITAT AND HABITS** Occurs in small parties, with individuals darting here and there to follow one another in gardens, scrub and grassland along forest edge, in dry environments. **STATUS** Common resident.

Common Tailorbird ■ *Orthotomus sutorius* 12cm;
Dark-necked Tailorbird ■ *O. atrogularis* 13cm

DESCRIPTION Dark greenish wings, back and tail; chestnut cap, darker, duller, and merging more smoothly into back in Common than in Dark-throated; light variable streaking on sides of face and throat. Common always has chestnut thighs. Juveniles lack brown cap, but usually have brownish tinge on forehead. Dark-necked has striking blackish feathering on either side of neck. **DISTRIBUTION** Common across South and Southeast Asia down to Java. Dark-necked from Northeast India, across Myanmar, through Southeast Asia, Sumatra and Borneo. **HABITAT AND HABITS** Abundant garden birds, but also widespread in cultivation, plantations, scrub, roadsides and riverbanks. Call of Common a rapid, repeated *chikchikchik* … in monotonously prolonged bouts. Nests built by stitching big leaves together to form pouch. **STATUS** Common residents.

Common Tailorbird

Dark-necked Tailorbird

Brown Grasshopper-warbler ■ *Locustella luteoventris* 14cm

DESCRIPTION Plain but rather bright rufous-brown, brighter on flanks, darker on back and wings, with unmarked throat and buff undertail-coverts. Dark upper and pale lower mandibles.

DISTRIBUTION Eastern Himalaya into North and West Myanmar, and across southern China and northern Vietnam. **HABITAT AND HABITS** Found in scrub, grassland, other low vegetation and fallow hill rice, in higher hills to about 1,900m, lower in non-breeding season. Active but skulking and hard to glimpse well, but easily heard from its rhythmic, machine-like clicking, *tiktiktiktiktiktiktik.* Easily heard in Natmataung Natonal Park. **STATUS** Locally common resident.

Red-rumped Swallow ■ *Cecropis daurica* 17cm

DESCRIPTION Dark blue crown and wings, and deeply forked tail; sides of face and underparts mealy-white, narrowly streaked blackish. Distinct square patch on rump (and, depending on race, patch on nape), orange-rufous in adults, buff in juveniles.

DISTRIBUTION Resident across Old World from Spain to Himalaya, Japan and Korea. Resident in hills in most of Myanmar, ranging into central and south lowlands during winter. **HABITAT AND HABITS** Has become more common over past 30–40 years. Occurs from sea-level mangroves, to 1,250m over forested mountains, but mostly in open coastal plains, cultivation, grassland and scrub. Occasional birds can be distinguished from wintering Barn Swallows (opposite) by more deliberate flight, and obvious rump colour. **STATUS** Uncommon resident and winter visitor.

Wire-tailed Swallow ■ *Hirundo smithii* 14cm, plus long tail streamers;
Barn Swallow ■ *H. rustica* 17cm

DESCRIPTION Dark glossy blue, almost black above, whitish below. Wire-tailed small with chestnut crown (paler in juveniles), pure white throat and underparts, and very long outer-tail feathers. Barn larger but shorter tailed, with rufous forehead, face and throat, and may show buffy-white to pink underparts, seldom pure white. **DISTRIBUTION** Barn worldwide, breeding in temperate areas and wintering in tropics and southern hemisphere. Wire-tailed in tropical Africa, South Asia and North, Central and South lowlands in Myanmar, into mainland Southeast Asia. **HABITAT AND HABITS** Both hawk for insects in skies over open country from lowlands to about 2,000m, Barn more often in drier areas, cultivation and settlements; Wire-tailed over rivers and lakes. **STATUS** Breeds in North and commonly winters throughout (Barn); uncommon along large rivers (Wire-tailed).

Wire-tailed Swallow

Barn Swallow

Asian Plain Martin ■ *Riparia chinensis* 11cm

DESCRIPTION Small, fawn-coloured martin, with tail hardly forked and lacking any breast-band; greyish-fawn on throat gradually fading down underparts to whitish vent; rump slightly paler than rest of back. Crown not contrasting with face and throat. **DISTRIBUTION** Through South and Southeast Asia, to Taiwan and the Philippines. **HABITAT AND HABITS** Found in lowlands and hills to about 1,220m, hawking for insects in groups, often among other swallows and martins, particularly near rivers and lakes. Breeds along sandbanks in all main rivers in Myanmar. **STATUS** Locally abundant resident.

Black Bulbul ■ *Hypsipetes leucocephalus* 23–26cm

DESCRIPTION All-grey, shaggy-headed bulbul with red bill, legs and skin around eye; grey plumage differs in shade between races. Entire head and throat, and even upper breast, immaculate white in some migrant races. Juveniles similar to adults but duller, brown, with duller bill and legs. **DISTRIBUTION** Himalaya through southern China and Southeast Asia. Throughout Myanmar. **HABITAT AND HABITS** Sometimes found singly but often in large groups, in mixed evergreen and deciduous forests, in hills at 500–3,000m. Winter migrants lower and in wider range of tree habitats. **STATUS** Common resident and winter visitor.

Black-crested Bulbul
■ *Pycnonotus flaviventris* 19cm

DESCRIPTION Dull olive-green above, olive-yellow below, with entire head and throat black; iris cream, and black vertical crest. **DISTRIBUTION** Resident from central Himalayan foothills and Indian subcontinent through Southeast Asia. Throughout Myanmar. **HABITAT AND HABITS** Occurs in lowlands, foothills and slopes in forests. Single or in pairs, flying out to snap at passing insects, and taking varied small fruits including figs. Breeds roughly January–July. Nests in dense forest-edge creepers and bracken. **STATUS** Common resident.

Red-whiskered Bulbul ■ *Pycnonotus jocosus* 19cm

DESCRIPTION Vertical black crest, white cheeks with red flash behind eye, and red undertail-coverts distinctive. Largely white below and brown above with narrow moustache-stripe. Sexes alike.
DISTRIBUTION Naturally resident throughout Myanmar, and from India to Hainan and Indochina, but heavily traded and trapped along Thai border in East and South Myanmar.
HABITAT AND HABITS Where not endangered by trapping can be abundant, feeding on fruits from range of garden and forest-edge plants as well as insects, occasionally coming to the ground for food. Nest a large cup of grass and creepers, hidden in dense foliage.
STATUS Common resident.

Red-vented Bulbul
■ *Pycnonotus cafer* 23cm

DESCRIPTION Medium-sized bulbul with dusky ear-patch on all-dark head. Rest of plumage above and below smoky grey-brown with paler feather-fringes; white rump and red undertail-coverts. Tail has narrow whitish tip. **DISTRIBUTION** Across Indian subcontinent, and into North, West, Central, East and South Myanmar. **HABITAT AND HABITS** Occurs in secondary scrub, tall bushes and overgrown cultivation, in lowlands to about 1,900m, often in pairs or small parties. **STATUS** Common resident.

Pale-eyed Bulbul
■ *Pycnonotus davisoni* 19–20cm

DESCRIPTION All-brown plumage, darker on back and wings, paler on breast, fading to grey then yellower belly to yellow undertail-coverts. Indistinct grey streaking on breast and short yellow streaks on head feathers; brighter yellowish-brown edges to wing feathers forming lighter panel. Iris pearly-grey. **DISTRIBUTION** Restricted to lowlands of West, South and Tenasserim, Myanmar. **HABITAT AND HABITS** Occurs in forest edges and secondary growth along roadsides or tracks in the few remaining forest patches in Ayeyarwady Delta, often in pairs. **STATUS** Endemic, locally uncommon resident restricted to small, localised area in the delta.

Ayeyarwady Bulbul ■ *Pycnonotus blanfordi* 18–20cm;
Streak-eared Bulbul ■ *P. conradi* 18–20cm

DESCRIPTION Medium-sized, rather featureless brown bulbuls, until recently considered a single species. In both ear-coverts finely streaked with white. Light olive-brown, a little paler below, and belly washed yellowish. In Streak-eared undertail-coverts tinged dirty yellow and eye pale grey; this colour much less evident in Ayeyarwady, which has red eye. **DISTRIBUTION** Ayeyarwady in West, Central, South and northern Tenasserim, Myanmar; Streak-eared in East along Mekong River, extending to Thailand and Indochina. **HABITAT AND HABITS** Found in secondary growth along roadsides in cultivation, gardens, forest edges and scrub in rather dry habitats. In lowlands to about 915m. **STATUS** Common residents.

Ayeyarwady Bulbul
Streak-eared Bulbul

White-headed Bulbul
■ *Cerasophila thompsoni* 20cm

DESCRIPTION Back and underparts light grey, wing and tail darker, and vent chestnut; head and neck white with black line through eye; bill and legs red. Like small version of white-headed populations of the Black Bulbul (p. 102), but paler grey body, black eye-line and chestnut vent distinctive. Juveniles nondescript light brown, head becoming paler. **DISTRIBUTION** Restricted to East and Tenasserim, Myanmar, into north Thailand. **HABITAT AND HABITS** Found in evergreen forest edges, secondary growth and scrub in hills, at about 900–2,100m. **STATUS** Near-endemic, uncommon resident.

Yellow-browed Warbler ■ *Phylloscopus inornatus* 11.5cm

DESCRIPTION Very small leaf-warbler with greenish crown, back, rump and tail, and broad whitish supercilium. Two wing-bars, slightly broader, particularly that on median wing-coverts. **DISTRIBUTION** Breeds across Palearctic, winters in Myanmar, and continues south to Peninsular Malaysia. **HABITAT AND HABITS** Found in trees in varied forest types, secondary growth, parks and gardens, from sea level to about 2,400m. **STATUS** Common winter visitor.

Ashy-throated Warbler ■ *Phylloscopus maculipennis* 9.5cm

DESCRIPTION Very small leaf-warbler with pale central crown-stripe, yellow rump and white sides to tail. Two white wing-bars, white supercilium and pale legs. White in tail

and greyish throat and upper breast important for identification. **DISTRIBUTION** Across Himalaya, to West, North and East Myanmar, into South China and northern Indochina. **HABITAT AND HABITS** Found in broadleaved evergreen forest in hilly country, typically above 1,500m, but descending to foothills outside breeding season. **STATUS** Locally common resident.

Dusky Warbler ■ *Phylloscopus fuscatus* 12cm

DESCRIPTION Small warbler with dusky grey-brown, unmarked crown, back, wings and tail; distinct white supercilium bordered dark below; underparts paler, washed buff

on flanks. Legs and lower mandible pale. **DISTRIBUTION** Breeds in eastern Palearctic, including Mongolia and northern China. Winters across Himalaya and southern China and Southeast Asia. Throughout Myanmar. **HABITAT AND HABITS** Found from sea level, mostly in lowlands but reaching above 1,800m, in any bushy-lined wetland areas. Presence often betrayed by hard clicking *teck* call. **STATUS** Common winter visitor.

Tickell's Leaf-warbler
■ *Phylloscopus affinis* 11cm;
Yellow-streaked Warbler
■ *P. armandii* 13cm

DESCRIPTION Small or medium warblers, both rather similar to the Dusky Warbler (opposite), but Tickell's greener above and yellower below and on supercilium, and Yellow-streaked browner with considerably richer buff flanks and breast, and breast feathers having yellowish central streaks. Supercilium less obvious in Tickell's, more obvious and whiter in Yellow-streaked. **DISTRIBUTION** Tickell's breeds across Himalaya into Central China, wintering to India and Myanmar. Yellow-streaked breeds through Central China, and winters into North, Central and South Myanmar, as well as northern Indochina. **HABITAT AND HABITS** Tickell's a bird of scrub in open country with scattered trees, from lowlands to above 2,100m. Call hard clicking *teck* similar to Dusky Warbler. Yellow-streaked also in low vegetation but prefers more trees, along forest edges and clearings in mixed forest, mostly breeding in montane forest above 1,200m, and wintering into lowlands. Calls with bunting-like tik, very different from other *Phylloscopus* in Myanmar. **STATUS** Uncommon winter visitors, often found around the temples in Bagan.

Tickell's Leaf-warbler

Yellow-streaked Warbler

Greenish Warbler
■ *Phylloscopus trochiloides* 13cm;

DESCRIPTION Light grey-green, paler below, usually with single, narrow, whitish wing-bar. Primaries, secondaries and tail feathers edged greenish, bright when in fresh plumage. **Two-barred Warbler** *P. plumbeitarsus* very similar but with two pale wing-bars, that on greater wing-coverts broad, yellower, that on median coverts short and narrow. **DISTRIBUTION** Breeds across western and central Palearctic, wintering in South and Southeast Asia, throughout Myanmar. **HABITAT AND HABITS** Occurs in evergreen forests in hills to above 2,500m. Greenish gives a *t'sli* call; Two-barred more disyllabic *tsi-z'li*. **STATUS** Common.

Chestnut-headed Tesia ■ *Cettia castaneocoronata* 9cm

DESCRIPTION Tiny, almost tailless bird with chestnut crown and face sharply defined against yellow throat and underside; olive-green wings and rump; very short tail. Whitish

crescent immediately behind eye. Juveniles similar but with dull brown back, wings, crown and face, and rufous-brown underparts. **DISTRIBUTION** Himalaya to hills of Southwest China and northern Southeast Asia, including North, West and East Myanmar. **HABITAT AND HABITS** Found in undergrowth, sometimes on the ground, in broadleaved evergreen forests in hills and mountains, at about 950–2,800m, lower outside breeding season. **STATUS** Uncommon resident.

Yellow-bellied Warbler ■ *Abroscopus superciliaris* 9cm;
Rufous-faced Warbler ■ *A. albogularis* 8–9cm

DESCRIPTION Yellow-bellied has grey-brown crown and sides of face; greenish back, wings and tail; whitish eyebrow and breast, becoming yellow from lower breast to vent. Rufous-faced has blackish-streaked brow and throat, and rufous sides of face. Sexes alike, and juveniles paler than adults, with less distinct brow and face pattern. **DISTRIBUTION** Yellow-bellied from eastern Himalaya to China, Greater Sundas. Throughout Myanmar. Rufous-faced from Himalaya to South China and Taiwan. North, West and East Myanmar. **HABITAT AND HABITS** Characteristic of bamboo in hilly forest at 500–1,500m (Yellow-bellied), or 1,800m (Rufous-faced), singly or in pairs or small parties. Often forage among bamboo but also in other trees in middle storey. **STATUS** Locally uncommon residents.

Yellow-bellied Warbler

Rufous-faced Warbler

Black-throated Tit ■ *Aegithalos concinnus* 11cm;
Burmese Tit ■ *A. bonvaloti sharpei* 11cm

DESCRIPTION Small and long-tailed, with tiny bill but rather large-headed appearance. Both have broad black mask from bill to nape, and grey crown, wings and tail. Black-throated has central black throat-patch bordered below by white, then narrow, deep chestnut breast-band. Burmese has broader mask, and speckled throat-patch with narrow white border, then more diffuse cinnamon breast-band with cinnamon flush on sides of face. **DISTRIBUTION** Resident from Northeast India, across North and East Myanmar, to Central and Southeast China. Burmese only in Chin Hills, especially Natmataung National Park. **HABITAT AND HABITS** Found respectively at 900–2,600m and 1,800–3,100m, in small flocks in hilly and montane broadleaved evergreen forests, mixed and coniferous forests and disturbed edges. **STATUS** Locally common residents.

Black-throated Tit

Burmese Tit

Yellow-eyed Babbler ■ *Chrysomma sinense* 17–19cm

DESCRIPTION Brown above and white below, washed with grey-buff on flanks and belly; whiter on sides of face continuing in front of eye to join with white brow. Rather staring yellow eye, surrounded by red skin. Short, robust black bill and long, graduated tail. **DISTRIBUTION** Resident in South and mainland Southeast Asia north of Isthmus of Kra. Through North, Central, West, East and South Myanmar. **HABITAT AND HABITS** Found in lowlands to above 1,800m, in secondary growth, scrub and grassland. Rather secretive but can be vocal. Often in pairs or small family groups. **STATUS** Common resident.

Jerdon's Babbler ■ *Chrysomma altirostre* 16–17cm

DESCRIPTION Slightly smaller than the Yellow-eyed Babbler (p. 109), with greyer breast and warmer brownish flanks and sides of face; eye darker amber or brown, with traces of darker eye-line. Bill horn coloured with paler lower mandible. **DISTRIBUTION** Great rivers of South Asia and Myanmar – Indus, Brahmaputra and Ayeyarwady. **HABITAT AND HABITS** Found in lowlands, in tall riverine grassland. Softer, lower and less varied songs than in Yellow-eyed. **STATUS** Locally uncommon resident, lost in Myanmar from beginning of Second World War until rediscovery in 2014. Population being reduced by expansion of intensive agriculture and burning to produce fresh fodder, drastically fragmenting riverine grassland.

Pale-billed Parrotbill ■ *Chleuasicusatro superciliaris* 15cm

DESCRIPTION Small but fairly large headed with stubby pink bill. Rufous-brown above; brighter cinnamon on crown, neck and nape; crown feathers raised into a little crest; small, black crescent-shaped brow behind eye. Nearly white below from throat to vent. **DISTRIBUTION** Eastern Himalaya, through North, West and East Myanmar, into northern Indochina. **HABITAT AND HABITS** Occurs in hilly land at 500–2,000m, sometimes down to 200m, in secondary growth, especially bamboo at forest edges. Found in small flocks, often mixed foraging flocks with other parrotbill species. **STATUS** Uncommon resident.

Whiskered Yuhina ■ *Yuhina flavicollis* 13cm

DESCRIPTION Grey face, with peaked crest on crown, separated from brown back and wings by rufous-buff half-collar. Blackish moustache-streak, and underparts white, with faint streaks on upper breast and white streaks on greyish flanks. **DISTRIBUTION** Resident from Himalaya, to North, West and East Myanmar, into northern Indochina. **HABITAT AND HABITS** Occurs in hills at about 1,200–2,600m in north, coming lower during non-breeding season, to 200m. Found in evergreen forests, forest edges and associated secondary regrowth, in small, active flocks. **STATUS** Common resident.

Burmese Yuhina ■ *Yuhina humilis* 13cm

DESCRIPTION Like Whiskered Yuhina (above), similarly crested, but with darker brownish face, pale grey half-collar between nape and back, and more pronounced white streaking on slightly greyer breast and flanks. **DISTRIBUTION** Resident in East Myanmar, especially Shan Yoma and hills into north-west Thailand. **HABITAT AND HABITS** Found in hills at about 1,050–2300m, coming lower during non-breeding season. Occurs in evergreen forests, forest edges and associated secondary regrowth. Seen in small, active flocks, including mixed foraging flocks; individuals keep in touch with continual calling. **STATUS** Near-endemic, uncommon resident. Serious decline due to habitat loss in its Myanmar range.

Indian White-eye ■ *Zosterops palpebrosus* 11cm

DESCRIPTION Small, olive-green above, yellow on throat, breast and flanks, and variably yellow on forehead; flanks greyer and belly white. Clear ring of white around

eye. Black bill and legs. **DISTRIBUTION** Resident in South and Southeast Asia. Throughout Myanmar. **HABITAT AND HABITS** Found in mangroves, gardens, cultivation with abundant trees, and evergreen and deciduous forests, from sea level to above 1,500m. Active, in flocks, gleaning insects from foliage. **STATUS** Uncommon resident.

Chin Hills Wren-babbler ■ *Spelaeornis oatesi* 12cm

DESCRIPTION Small, fairly short-tailed, dark brown above on back, wings and tail, and speckled crown and face; white or slightly grey background colour below, speckled black

on breast, and more thickly on sides of neck, breast and flanks. **DISTRIBUTION** Resident in West Myanmar, through Chin Hills, along shared border with Manipur and Mizoram. Regularly found in Natmataung National Park. **HABITAT AND HABITS** Occurs in undergrowth in and near forests in hills, at about 1,400–2800m, in broadleaved evergreen vegetation and forest edges. Hard to see well but vocal, uttering rapid, simple but undulating phrases, perhaps including duets. **STATUS** Near-endemic, locally common resident.

Grey-bellied Wren-babbler ■ *Spelaeornis reptatus* 10cm

DESCRIPTION Like the Chin Hills Wren-babbler (opposite), but sides of face grey, throat white and rest of underparts more thickly scaled (rather than spotted) with black and white on warm buffy-brown background, especially on sides of breast and flanks. **DISTRIBUTION** Resident in North and East Myanmar along border with Yunnan. **HABITAT AND HABITS** Found in undergrowth in and near forests in hills, at about 1,400–2,800m, in broadleaved evergreen vegetation and forest edges. Hard to see well but vocal, uttering repeated descending trills, perhaps including duets. **STATUS** Locally uncommon resident.

Slender-billed Scimitar-babbler ■ *Pomatorhinus superciliaris* 20cm

DESCRIPTION Dark brown above and warm rufous-buff below, darkening steadily from whitish throat to dark vent. Head darker with poor white supercilium, and bill very long, downcurved and black. **DISTRIBUTION** Resident in central and eastern Himalaya, through North, West and East Myanmar, Yunnan and north Indochina. **HABITAT AND HABITS** Occurs from foothills to mountains, at about 900–2,750m, in broadleaved evergreen forests and bamboo regrowth. Utters long series of clear, piping calls, one delivered very fast, another similar but slower. **STATUS** Locally uncommon resident.

White-browed Scimitar-babbler ■ *Pomatorhinus schisticeps* 22cm;
Streak-breasted Scimitar-babbler ■ *P. ruficollis* 18–19cm

DESCRIPTION Both rich brown above, from crown to tail; sides of face darker, with clear white supercilium. Underparts largely white in White-browed; in slightly smaller Streak-breasted, throat white but remainder of underparts heavily streaked with chestnut-brown. Bill mostly yellow with black on upper mandible; eye yellow. **DISTRIBUTION** Resident in Himalaya and mainland Southeast Asia. Streak-breasted in West, North and East Myanmar; White-browed more widespread, continuing into Central, South and Tenasserim. **HABITAT AND HABITS** Respectively in broadleaved evergreen forests to about 2,400m, or evergreen and deciduous forests at about 900–2,100m. Both species can be highly vocal. **STATUS** Common residents.

White-browed Scimitar-babbler   *Streak-breasted Scimitar-babbler*

Grey-throated Babbler ■ *Stachyris nigriceps* 13–14cm

DESCRIPTION Dark brown back, wings and tail; more ochre-buff cheeks, breast and belly, with subdued pattern of white eyebrow and white malar patch imposed over grey crown; grey throat; blackish around and in front of eye. **DISTRIBUTION** Resident from eastern Himalaya, through southern China and continental Southeast Asia, to Sumatra and Borneo. **HABITAT AND HABITS** Insectivore: busy groups of 4–5 work through dense undergrowth, fern brakes and vegetation of forested roadsides and landslips, in lowland and montane evergreen forests, on slopes from just above sea level to beyond 2,000m. Continual tremulous, reeling trills between flock members. **STATUS** Common resident.

Chestnut-capped Babbler ▪ *Timalia pileata* 18cm

DESCRIPTION Like the Yellow-eyed Babbler (p. 109), but with clear white forehead joining supercilium, and dark eye with black eye-line meeting base of bill; throat white, grading to buff breast and belly. Bill black in adults, black with pale lower mandible in juveniles. **DISTRIBUTION** Resident along foothills of Himalaya and through continental Southeast Asia. Throughout Myanmar. **HABITAT AND HABITS** Occurs in secondary vegetation, grassland and scrub, from lowlands to about 1,500m. Small groups travel inconspicuously, giving range of squeaky and harsh contact calls. **STATUS** Uncommon resident.

Pin-striped Tit-babbler ▪ *Mixornis gularis* 12cm

DESCRIPTION Small, with rufous crown, yellowish eyebrow, face and underparts, and throat and upper breast finely streaked with dark brown; back olive-brown, more rufous on wings and tail; face pale yellowish, with bare light skin around eyes. **DISTRIBUTION** India across continental Southeast Asia, to Java, Bali, Borneo and Palawan, with more easterly birds possibly a separate species. Throughout Myanmar. **HABITAT AND HABITS** Found in scrubby secondary growth, farmland, plantations and forest edges. Presence often given away by repeated *chonkchonkchonk*, often in clusters of 3–4 notes (one sex), or harsh sizzling *shrrrt-shree* (the other sex). **STATUS** Common resident.

Variable Limestone Babbler ■ *Gypsophila crispifrons* 18–20cm

DESCRIPTION Cool, dark, greyish-brown above, mottled darker; longer tail than in other wren-babblers; no pale spots on wing-coverts. Boldly streaked black on buffy-white from throat to lower breast, fading to cold grey-brown belly. Some birds west of Thanlwin (Salween) River show variable amount of white on head and breast. **DISTRIBUTION** Resident in karst landscapes of northern Tenasserim, Myanmar, into western Thailand. **HABITAT AND HABITS** Closely associated with karst limestone hills in lowlands. Small groups occur within forests on and around the foot of such crags, to about 900m. **STATUS** Locally common resident.

White form

Puff-throated Babbler ■ *Pellorneum ruficeps* 17cm

DESCRIPTION Bright brown cap separated from brown back and slightly greyer-brown face by long buff supercilium, almost reaching nape. Underparts very pale buff, strongly

streaked blackish on breast and flanks. Juveniles more rufous than adults, but with much less streaking on underparts. **DISTRIBUTION** Resident in South and Southeast Asia. Throughout Myanmar. **HABITAT AND HABITS** Occurs on the ground or in undergrowth, particularly in bamboo, as well as secondary vegetation, and evergreen and deciduous forest edges, in lowlands to about 1,800m. **STATUS** Common resident.

Brown-cheeked Fulvetta ■ *Alcippe poiocephala* 16cm

DESCRIPTION Plain, light brown back and wings; underside entirely plain buffy-white; sides of face buffy-grey; crown ash-grey. Depending on location, variably distinct narrow black brow from bill to nape, almost invisible in some populations. **DISTRIBUTION** Resident in South and Southeast Asia. Throughout Myanmar. **HABITAT AND HABITS** Found in lowlands and hills to above 1,200m, occasionally to 1,500m, in broadleaved evergreen and deciduous forests. In lower storey, small foraging flocks. **STATUS** Common resident.

Nepal Fulvetta
■ *Alcippe nipalensis* 16cm

DESCRIPTION Like the Brown-cheeked Fulvetta (above), but with all colours a little deeper, and brighter rufous upperparts, sides of face distinctly grey showing greater contrast with pale throat, and underparts more buff. White lore and white eye-ring. **DISTRIBUTION** Resident in North and West Myanmar, across Himalaya. **HABITAT AND HABITS** Found in hills and mountains at 400m to almost 2,500m, in broadleaved evergreen forests, forest edges and associated secondary growth. In lower storey, small foraging flocks. **STATUS** Common resident.

Striated Babbler ■ *Turdoides earlei* 21–22cm

DESCRIPTION Long-tailed babbler with narrow brown streaks. Dark brown crown, back, wings and faintly barred tail; all but tail and flight feathers have darker streaks. Buffy-brown below, warmest on breast with narrow dark streaks. Bill yellowish with dark tip and ridge. **DISTRIBUTION** Resident along large rivers from Indus to Ayeyarwady, across foothills of Himalaya. Central, South-west and South Myanmar. **HABITAT AND HABITS** Small flocks occur in lowlands, in grass and scrub, often near water. Group members call loudly to one another. **STATUS** Locally uncommon resident.

Adult   *Adult*

White-throated Babbler ■ *Chatarrhaea gularis* 25cm (e)

DESCRIPTION Long-tailed babbler with rich rufous-brown head, breast and underparts; sides of face sharply defined from white throat. Back, wings and faintly barred tail dark

brown; back streaked darker. Eye yellowish-white. **DISTRIBUTION** Restricted to dry zone, North, Central and South Myanmar; regularly seen around temples of Bagan and gardens of Mandalay and Naypyidaw. **HABITAT AND HABITS** Occurs in lowlands to about 600m, in scrub and grassland associated with cultivation in dry central core of Myanmar. Members of flock keep in continual vocal contact. **STATUS** Endemic, common resident.

White-crested Laughingthrush ■ *Garrulax leucolophus* 26–30cm

DESCRIPTION Back, wings, rump, tail and flanks rich rufous-brown, unmarked; head, crest, throat and upper breast (and in some populations reaching to belly) white. Black mask through eye. **DISTRIBUTION** Resident in Himalaya. Throughout Myanmar to continental Southeast Asia. **HABITAT AND HABITS** Found from lowlands to above 1,600m, occasionally to above 2,100m, in broadleaved evergreen and deciduous forests. Occurs in small, occasionally large, noisy flocks, in middle to lower storeys. **STATUS** Common resident.

White-browed Laughingthrush ■ *Garrulax sannio* 22–24cm

DESCRIPTION Plain warm brown, a little richer on crown and throat, and more rufous on undertail-coverts; distinctive buffy-white eyebrows and cheeks, meeting in front of eye. **DISTRIBUTION** Resident in North and East Myanmar, across South China and north Indochina. **HABITAT AND HABITS** Occurs in hilly land at about 600m to above 1,800m, in small, noisy flocks in secondary forests, bamboo, scrub and grassland with scattered bushes or trees. **STATUS** Common resident.

Mount Victoria Babax
■ *Garrulax woodi* 23–26cm

DESCRIPTION Large, streaky, long-tailed laughingthrush. Dark brown streaks on buffy-white background, with blackish streaks on crown, back and undersides from throat to belly. Pale eye. Streaking less heavy in juveniles than adults. **DISTRIBUTION** Resident in West Myanmar, the Chin Hills into Mizoram. **HABITAT AND HABITS** Occurs in pairs or small parties, in hilly areas at 1,200–2,800m, in broadleaved evergreen forests, forest edges and associated secondary vegetation, in lower storey or coming to ground in open areas like grassland. **STATUS** Near-endemic, uncommon resident.

Brown-capped Laughingthrush ■ *Trochalopteron austeni* 24cm

DESCRIPTION Warm brown above, more rufous on flight feathers; tips of wing-coverts,

secondaries and tail tipped whitish; head speckled, slightly darker on face; underparts buffy-white thickly scaled with brown. **DISTRIBUTION** Resident in North and West Myanmar along border with Nagaland, Manipur and Mizoram. **HABITAT AND HABITS** Found from below 2,000m to above 3,000m in montane oak and rhododendrons, forest edges and associated secondary vegetation. Noisy but difficult to see well. Usually single or in pairs. **STATUS** Near-endemic, locally common resident.

Striped Laughingthrush ■ *Trochalopteron virgatum* 23cm

DESCRIPTION Warm brown; brighter rufous on greater wing-coverts and secondaries, and on throat. Most of head and body has profuse narrow white streaks; broad whitish eyebrow and moustache.
DISTRIBUTION Resident in North and West Myanmar along border with Nagaland, Manipur and Mizoram.
HABITAT AND HABITS Found in hills and montane zone at 1,400–2,400m, in forest edges, secondary growth, bamboo and grassland. Usually in pairs, often duetting; difficult to see well. **STATUS** Near-endemic, uncommon resident.

Grey Sibia

■ *Heterophasia gracilis* 23–25cm

DESCRIPTION Predominantly ashy-grey and white. Nearly black on head, the colour merging into grey back but sharply cut off from white throat and underparts. In flight, shows grey and black wing-panels, and black edges and subterminal bar to tail. **DISTRIBUTION** Resident in North and West Myanmar along border with Northeast India. **HABITAT AND HABITS** Found in hills and montane zone at 1,400–2,800m, in broadleaved evergreen forests including oak and chestnut. In small flocks. **STATUS** Common resident.

Silver-eared Mesia ▪ *Leiothrix argentauris* 17cm

DESCRIPTION Very colourful with black head, silvery-white ear-coverts, yellow forehead, nape, collar and breast, and yellow in wing. Wings otherwise grey with reddish bases to

flight feathers; rump and undertail-coverts reddish in male, yellow in female. **DISTRIBUTION** Resident from central Himalaya to Malaysia and Sumatra, through North, West, East and Tenasserim, Myanmar. **HABITAT AND HABITS** Small, noisy parties surge through understorey, giving whistled eight-note song, *tee-oo-wit, tee-oo-wit, tee-oo*, and other varied notes. Regional differences in song between populations. Occurs in canopy of forest, at 900–2,000m, and down into fern brakes and scrub in old cultivation, occasionally to below 400m. **STATUS** Common resident.

Rusty-fronted Barwing ▪ *Actinodura egertoni* 21–23cm;
Spectacled Barwing ▪ *A. ramsayi* 22–24cm

DESCRIPTION Warm buffy-brown, with greyer face and regular black barring across wings and tail. In Rusty-fronted forehead, throat and wing-coverts rufous, and rear of head grey; Spectacled has blackish lores contrasting with white eye-ring. **DISTRIBUTION** Rusty-fronted resident across central and eastern Himalaya into North and West Myanmar. Spectacled from East Myanmar and north-west Thailand to northern Indochina and southern Yunnan. **HABITAT AND HABITS** Occur in mostly hilly land at 1,000–2,600m, lower in winter; Rusty-fronted occasionally to 250m or lower. Found in broadleaved evergreen forests, forest edges and associated secondary growth; Spectacled even in tussocky grass. **STATUS** Uncommon residents.

Rusty-fronted Barwing

Spectacled Barwing

Bar-tailed Treecreeper ▪ *Certhia himalayana* 14cm

DESCRIPTION Small, dark brown above, streaked paler on crown, back, wings and coverts; wing feathers crossed by zones of brown and grey. Whitish below with white supercilium and long, curved bill. Differs from other treecreepers by light grey-brown tail crossed by about 10 narrow but distinct black bars. **DISTRIBUTION** Resident across Himalaya into Southwest China. North and West Myanmar. **HABITAT AND HABITS** Occurs in mountains at above 2,100–3,000m, in broadleaved, mixed and coniferous forests. Creeps up tree trunks and larger branches. **STATUS** Uncommon resident.

Burmese Nuthatch
▪ *Sitta neglecta* 13cm

DESCRIPTION 'Typical' nuthatch with grey upperparts, buff underparts strengthening from nearly white throat to rufous flanks, and black line through eye. Undertail-coverts scaled with white. Tone of upperparts and underparts, and tail-covert pattern, are key points. **DISTRIBUTION** North, West, East and South Myanmar, across northern Thailand, to central and southern Indochina. **HABITAT AND HABITS** Found in lowlands to above 1,500m, in dry mixed and pine forests, creeping down tree trunks. Often among mixed foraging flocks. **STATUS** Uncommon resident.

White-browed Nuthatch ■ *Sitta victoriae* 11.5cm

DESCRIPTION Small, rather pale nuthatch. Face and most of underparts white; cinnamon flanks and plain undertail-coverts. Tail has incomplete white band. Lores white, as black

eye-line (bordered above by white line) does not extend to bill. **DISTRIBUTION** Restricted to Mt Victoria in West Myanmar, in Natmataung National Park. **HABITAT AND HABITS** Found in montane forests of oak, chestnut and rhododendrons, at 2,500–2,800m when breeding, to below 2,300m outside breeding season. **STATUS** Endemic, uncommon resident. Tiny range threatened by habitat loss through seasonal burning, and habitat may continue to decline due to climate change.

Beautiful Nuthatch ■ *Sitta formosa* 16cm

DESCRIPTION Upperparts black; feathers tipped with deep azure-blue on crown, back,

coverts and wings; wing feathers and greater coverts edged white. Narrow black eye-line, pale supercilium, whitish sides of face and throat darkening to rufous buff on breast and belly. **DISTRIBUTION** Resident from eastern Himalaya, through North, West and East Myanmar, to northern Indochina. **HABITAT AND HABITS** Found in hills and mountains at 700–2,300m, in broadleaved evergreen and semi-evergreen forests. Often among mixed foraging flocks. **STATUS** Locally uncommon resident. Vulnerable due to continuing forest loss.

Asian Pied Starling
■ *Gracupica contra* 22–25cm

DESCRIPTION Strikingly pied black and white; upperparts largely black with white band across scapulars and mantle; black chin and throat sharply defined against white underparts; white forehead and sides of face. Eye, bill and legs yellow; bill-base red and narrow ring of red skin around eye. **DISTRIBUTION** Resident in South and Southeast Asia. Throughout Myanmar. **HABITAT AND HABITS** Occurs in urban, suburban and agricultural areas in lowlands, open country, riversides and rice fields. Forages largely on the ground. **STATUS** Common resident.

Chestnut-tailed Starling ■ *Sturnia malabarica* 18–20cm

DESCRIPTION Ashy-grey above, paler and nearly white on head and all underparts; white flash at bend of wing; chestnut-brown outer-tail feathers. In some populations underparts flushed with chestnut, light on breast and darker towards vent. Bill yellow with blue base. Eyes and legs yellow. **DISTRIBUTION** Resident in South and Southeast Asia. Throughout Myanmar, travelling into Tenasserim in winter. **HABITAT AND HABITS** Found in lowlands and hills to 1,450m, in open country with scattered trees, copses and forest edges, usually in flocks. Forages largely off the ground, in trees, for insects, fruits and nectar. **STATUS** Common resident.

Common Myna ■ *Acridotheres tristis* 25cm;
Burmese Myna ■ *A. burmannicus* 22–25cm

DESCRIPTION Common smooth cinnamon-brown; head nearly black; yellow bill and bare yellow skin around dark eye. White vent, large white wing-patch and white tips to tail. In moult, some birds have entirely bare, scrawny yellow head. Burmese far paler, with light head and rump, and black around eye. **DISTRIBUTION** Common resident from Central to Southeast Asia. Throughout Myanmar. Burmese resident in Central, South and East Myanmar, barely extending into Yunnan. **HABITAT AND HABITS** Both occur in open country, scrub, cultivation and even city gardens, foraging mostly on the ground and on lawns; Burmese to a lesser extent in trees. Seen singly or in pairs, congregating at food sources, and in big communal roosts. **STATUS** Common resident (Common); near-endemic, common resident (Burmese).

Common Myna

Burmese Myna

Jungle Myna ■ *Acridotheres fuscus* 25cm

DESCRIPTION Largely ashy-brown myna, best told from very similar species by hard-to-

see blue base to orange-yellow bill, very short crest above bill and smallness of white patch at base of primaries (more visible in flight, also revealing relatively pale grey underwing). **DISTRIBUTION** Resident in South Asia. Through North, Central, West, South and Tenasserim, Myanmar, south to Peninsular Malaysia. **HABITAT AND HABITS** Found in lowlands, occasionally as high as 1,500m. Mostly in rural areas, gardens and agriculture, favouring scrub, orchards and scattered trees often near rivers and other waterbodies. **STATUS** Common resident.

Collared Myna ■ *Acridotheres albocinctus* 25cm;
Great Myna ■ *A. grandis* 27cm

DESCRIPTION Dark grey mynas, Collared having broad but incomplete whitish collar, small white wing-patch, and dark undertail-coverts with white scaling. Adult Great has shaggy crest on forecrown, larger white wing-patch, and undertail-coverts white (adult) or dark with whitish scaling (juvenile). Bill and eye ivory (Collared), or bill yellow and eye red (Great). Juveniles browner than adults, with shorter crests. **DISTRIBUTION** Collared resident in North, West and East Myanmar, barely overlapping into Northeast India and Yunnan. Great resident from Northeast India throughout Myanmar and continental Southeast Asia. **HABITAT AND HABITS** Found in lowlands and hills, occasionally to above 1,500m, in agricultural land, fallow, open country and grassland. Forages mainly on the ground. **STATUS** Near-endemic, common resident (Collared); common resident (Great).

Collared Myna

Great Myna

Green Cochoa ■ *Cochoa viridis* 28cm

DESCRIPTION Beautifully particoloured with blue crown and nape, and sage-green body; back has black feather-fringes; wing-coverts, flight feathers and tail azure-blue broadly tipped with black. Juveniles have similar but browner wing pattern, and head and body boldly spotted and barred with black on buff background. **DISTRIBUTION** Nomadic frugivore ranging from Northeast India, through North, West, East and north Tenasserim, Myanmar, into continental Southeast Asia. **HABITAT AND HABITS** Occurs in hills and montane zones at around 700–2,600m, lower outside breeding season, in middle storey of broadleaved evergreen forests. **STATUS** Rare nomadic resident.

Orange-headed Thrush ■ *Geokichla citrina* 21cm

DESCRIPTION Rich rufous-orange head and underparts, with back, wings and tail dark grey (in male) or olive-brown (in female), and white bar on bend of wing. Significant

variations in richness of orange plumage, whiteness or even presence of wing-bar, and of vertical dark bars on face characteristic of juveniles. **DISTRIBUTION** Resident and local migrant in South and Southeast Asia into South China, and south to Java and Bali. Throughout Myanmar. **HABITAT AND HABITS** On migration and wintering, occurs at any elevation from extreme lowlands upwards to montane forests, in heavily shaded, closed canopy conditions. Forages on the ground, hopping in leaf litter in forests, parks and gardens. **STATUS** Uncommon resident and winter visitor.

Black-breasted Thrush ■ *Turdus dissimilis* 23cm

DESCRIPTION Male has black head, throat and upper breast, sharply defining rufous flanks and white belly; dark grey wings, back and tail. In female upperparts and head

brown, throat and upper breast pale with heavy dark speckling, and flanks paler rufous. **DISTRIBUTION** Resident from Northeast India, through North, West and East Myanmar, into southern China and northern Indochina. **HABITAT AND HABITS** Occurs in hill and montane zone at 1,200–2,500m, in broadleaved evergreen, oak and coniferous forests; lower outside breeding season, down to 200m. **STATUS** Locally uncommon resident.

Eyebrowed Thrush ■ *Turdus obscurus* 23cm;
Grey-sided Thrush ■ *T. feae* 23.5cm

DESCRIPTION Unspotted brown thrushes with pale supercilium and dark line in front of eye. Male Eyebrowed has pale grey head, peachy upper breast and flanks, and white belly. Grey-sided has brown head, colder brown back and wings, and greyer underparts with a little streaking on throat. Female and young Eyebrowed tend to have slightly darker moustache-streak, bordered whitish below. **DISTRIBUTION** Eyebrowed breeds in eastern Palearctic, wintering across Southeast Asia. Grey-sided breeds in Northeast China, wintering in West and East Myanmar, into north Indochina. **HABITAT AND HABITS** Found at about 500–3,100m (Eyebrowed), or 500–2,500m (Grey-sided), in broadleaved evergreen forests in hills and mountains; Eyebrowed also occurs lower on migration, extending into secondary growth, parks and gardens. **STATUS** Locally common winter visitors. Vulnerable due to habitat loss in breeding and wintering areas.

Eyebrowed Thrush

Grey-sided Thrush

Oriental Magpie-robin
■ *Copsychus saularis* 20cm

DESCRIPTION Male has glossy black head, breast, back and wings, and white-sided tail; pure white belly and strong white wing-bar. Female more subdued grey and cream with wing-bar. **DISTRIBUTION** Resident in Indian subcontinent to southern China, through Southeast Asia to Greater Sundas. Throughout Myanmar. **HABITAT AND HABITS** Garden bird with fine, varied song given by male or both sexes from prominent perch; also in plantations, secondary woodland, forested riverbanks and mangroves. Drops to the ground for insects, worms and small vertebrates. **STATUS** Common resident.

White-rumped Shama ■ *Kittacincla malabarica* 21–28cm

DESCRIPTION Blue-glossed black head, breast, back, wings and tail; rufous belly; white rump and white edges to long tail. Female has same pattern as male, but duller and shorter-tailed. Juveniles have buff

wing-spots. **DISTRIBUTION** Resident from central Himalayan foothills, patchily through southern China south to Greater Sundas. Throughout Myanmar. **HABITAT AND HABITS** Favours understorey of lowland forests from sea level upwards, rarely to 1,200m, in lower montane zone, including overgrown plantations and secondary woodland. Like magpie-robins, persecuted by trapping because of fine, varied, sustained song. **STATUS** Common resident.

Asian Brown Flycatcher ■ *Muscicapa dauurica* 13.5cm

DESCRIPTION Nondescript grey-brown, with pale lores between bill and eye, and pale eye-ring; throat pale with no trace of extending backwards to form collar; breast pale grey-brown, sometimes with faint streaks. Black feet, and yellow base to lower mandible.

DISTRIBUTION Widespread, ranging through eastern Palearctic and wintering in South and Southeast Asia. Small resident population still poorly understood. **HABITAT AND HABITS** Seen singly, perched on conspicuous twig in middle or lower storey of forest edges, tree plantations and well-wooded parks, from sea level up to montane forests. Sits on bare twigs of trees or bushes, sallying out to snap up flies and mosquitoes, moths and other insects. **STATUS** Common localized breeder, winter visitor and migrant.

Verditer Flycatcher ■ *Eumyias thalassinus* 15–17cm

DESCRIPTION Bright light turquoise-blue throughout, with narrow black line from bill to just behind eye; slim black bill and legs. Female and non-breeding birds a little duller and greyer. **DISTRIBUTION** Resident in South and Southeast Asia, through to Greater Sundas. North, West, East and Tenasserim, Myanmar, though some migrate in winter or move down from higher elevations. **HABITAT AND HABITS** Found in lowlands and hills to above 2,700m, in clearings and edges of broadleaved evergreen forests, down to sea level, including gardens and even mangroves on migration. **STATUS** Uncommon resident.

Large Blue-flycatcher ■ *Cyornis magnirostris* 15cm

DESCRIPTION Male blue above and orange-rufous below extending on to flanks, with slightly paler throat and central white belly. Bill larger than in similar flycatchers, with minute amount of black on chin immediately below. Female light ashy-brown, very similar to other blue-flycatchers, but tail and wings slightly more rufous and bill larger. **DISTRIBUTION** Breeds in eastern Himalaya and North Myanmar, wintering in Tenasserim and Peninsular Malaysia. **HABITAT AND HABITS** Occurs in lowlands to 600m; to 1,200m in hills on migration. Favours broadleaved evergreen forests. **STATUS** Local northern breeder and rare winter visitor.

Indochinese Blue-flycatcher ■ *Cyornis sumatrensis* 14cm

DESCRIPTION Male blue above and orange-rufous below, not extending to flanks, with slightly paler throat. Bill small, with no black on chin. Female light ashy-brown above,

very similar to other blue-flycatchers, but upperparts have blue wash and flanks whitish. Both sexes have shorter wings than the Large Blue-flycatcher (p. 131). **DISTRIBUTION** Resident in East and Tenasserim, Myanmar, through Southeast Asia. **HABITAT AND HABITS** Found in lowlands to about 900m, in broadleaved evergreen, semi-evergreen and deciduous forests. **STATUS** Common resident. Previously included in *C. tickelliae*.

Siberian Rubythroat ■ *Calliope calliope* 15cm

DESCRIPTION Warm brown above from forehead and face to tail; underparts white, washed with grey-brown on breast and flanks. Male has white eyebrow, white moustache

and brilliant ruby-red throat edged with dark grey. Female lacks red throat but has similar if fainter eyebrow and moustache pattern on head. **DISTRIBUTION** Breeds across central and east Palearctic, wintering in South and Southeast Asia to Taiwan and the Philippines. Throughout Myanmar. **HABITAT AND HABITS** Habitat includes farmland with thick, weedy and grassy patches, hedges, secondary growth and woodland. Feeds largely on insects, on the ground. **STATUS** Common winter visitor.

Himalayan Bush-robin ■ *Tarsiger rufilatus* 14cm

DESCRIPTION Male blue above, with brighter blue brow, shoulder and rump; white throat, blue breast-sides and rufous-orange flanks. Female ashy-brown with blue rump and tail; below, narrow white throat-patch contrasting with greyish-brown wash on breast and whitish belly; washed out rufous-orange flanks. **DISTRIBUTION** Breeds through Himalaya into Southwest China. Winters into West and East Myanmar and northern Indochina. **HABITAT AND HABITS** Winters at hilly and montane elevations, 600m to above 3,600m, in lower storey of mixed birch, rhododendron and coniferous evergreen forests. **STATUS** Uncommon resident in North, and common winter visitor in West and East.

Black-backed Forktail ■ *Enicurus immaculatus* 21–23cm

DESCRIPTION Broad white forehead; black (not white or ashy-grey) crown and back; underparts white beginning on upper breast, with black confined to chin. Long, fork-tipped black and white tail. In juveniles, chin white, head and back dull brown, and no white forehead. **DISTRIBUTION** Resident from Himalaya through Northeast India, North, West, South-west, Central, East and South Myanmar, into north-west Thailand. **HABITAT AND HABITS** Often in pairs, along forest-lined rivers and rocky streams, in lowlands and hills to above 1,100m. **STATUS** Common resident.

White-crowned Forktail ■ *Enicurus leschenaulti* 28cm

DESCRIPTION Large forktail with white extending from forehead to beyond mid-crown; mantle, face and breast entirely black. White forehead feathers can be erected into peak.

Juveniles browner rather than black, also with dark breast. **DISTRIBUTION** Resident in Eastern Himalaya, South China, through Southeast Asia and Greater Sundas. Throughout Myanmar. **HABITAT AND HABITS** Occurs in lowlands, hills and mountains to 2,400m, along forested rivers and streams, extending away from rivers where forest is swampy. **STATUS** Common resident.

Blue Whistling-thrush ■ *Myophonus caeruleus* 32cm

DESCRIPTION Very big thrush, black all over with strong blue gloss with brighter blue spangles on wing-coverts and (depending on race) on back and breast. Bill black and

bright yellow in some races, feet grey. **DISTRIBUTION** Resident from Central Asia through Himalaya, into Central and East China, south Southeast Asia, to Sumatra and Java. Throughout Myanmar. **HABITAT AND HABITS** Found in forest edges, rocky rivers, near rocky outcrops, and even forest-edged road cuttings. Feeds on large common snails, leaving conspicuous middens of broken shells. Nests in rock crevices, even within cave mouths. **STATUS** Uncommon resident.

Taiga Flycatcher ■ *Ficedula albicilla* 13cm

DESCRIPTION Greyish-brown above, pale buffy-grey on breast, and whiter on throat, lower breast and belly; indistinct pale lores and eye-ring. Tail dark with white bases either

side. Breeding male has small, brick-red throat-patch with grey surround and sides of face. **DISTRIBUTION** Breeds in central and east Palearctic, wintering in South and Southeast Asia. Throughout Myanmar. **HABITAT AND HABITS** Found from lowlands to above 2,100m, in plantations, scrub, scattered trees, open woodland and forest edges; sometimes in parks and gardens. Often perches on tops of bushes. **STATUS** Common winter visitor.

White-capped Water-redstart ■ *Phoenicurus leucocephalus* 19cm

DESCRIPTION Dark with contrasting white crown from above forehead to nape; black forehead, face, back, wings and upper breast; rich rufous-chestnut lower breast and belly, rump and tail-base. Juveniles browner than adults; less contrast between brownish and rufous areas of plumage, and sullied whitish cap. **DISTRIBUTION** Resident across Himalaya and much of China into northern Southeast Asia. Breeds in North and West Myanmar, wintering in Central and East. **HABITAT AND HABITS** Occurs on boulders in rivers and streams, in hills and mountains, at about 900m to above 4,000m, lower in winter. **STATUS** Uncommon resident and winter visitor.

Plumbeous Water-redstart ■ *Phoenicurus fuliginosus* 15cm

DESCRIPTION Male dark bluish-grey except chestnut uppertail- and undertail-coverts and tail. Female light blue-grey above, scaly-grey below; browner face and wings, pale tips

to wing-coverts, and white patches either side of tail-base. **DISTRIBUTION** Resident across Himalaya and much of Central and East China, through North, West and East Myanmar, into northern Indochina. **HABITAT AND HABITS** Occurs on boulders in rivers and streams, in lowlands, hills and mountains, at about 300–2,300m, lower in winter. Moves down from hills and across lowlands in winter. **STATUS** Common resident and winter visitor.

Blue Rock-thrush ■ *Monticola solitarius* 22cm

DESCRIPTION Plain dark blue-grey. During breeding season variable light and dark, scale-like markings develop on body plumage. Migrant race has chestnut lower breast to

vent. Female light uniform scaly-brown all over. **DISTRIBUTION** Breeds across southern Palearctic and winters through tropical Africa, Middle East, South and Southeast Asia, to Indonesia. Populations may breed in North and south Tenasserim, and winter throughout Myanmar. **HABITAT AND HABITS** Residents most often near limestone and other cliffs; migrants anywhere, but often near buildings, roadside cuttings, dams or other exposed faces, or near seashore. **STATUS** Uncommon winter visitor.

Jerdon's Bushchat

■ *Saxicola jerdoni* 15cm

DESCRIPTION Male sharply defined black above and on sides of face; white below. Female light rufous-brown above and on sides of face; no supercilium; white on throat and belly; rest of underparts pale sandy-buff. **DISTRIBUTION** Resident from Northeast India to northern Indochina. North and East Myanmar; especially common on northern end of Inle Lake. **HABITAT AND HABITS** Occurs from lowlands to about 1,600m, hiding among dense scrub and thorn bushes, in grassland, along large and small rivers, or seasonally in dry river gullies. **STATUS** Locally common resident.

Pied Bushchat ■ *Saxicola caprata* 14cm

DESCRIPTION Male black with long white bar on upper wing, and white rump, uppertail-coverts and vent; plumage scaled with brown outside breeding season. Female lacks wing-bar; dark brown streaked with blackish; more rufous below, especially on vent, belly and rump. **DISTRIBUTION** Resident across South and Southeast Asia, through the Philippines and Wallacea, to Papua New Guinea. Breeds throughout Myanmar, south to northern Tenasserim. **HABITAT AND HABITS** Found from lowlands to about 1,600m, among dense grassland, scrub and second-growth bushes, sometimes perching prominently. **STATUS** Common resident.

White-tailed Stonechat ■ *Saxicola leucurus* 14cm;
Amur Stonechat ■ *S. stejnegeri* 14cm

DESCRIPTION Males have black hood, large white neck-patch, breast flushed rufous-buff, dark-streaked back and wings, and white wing-bar and rump. Females and non-breeding males light brown streaked darker above, with buff upper breast, pale throat and often traces of neck-patch. White-tailed in all plumages shows white bases to tail-sides. **DISTRIBUTION** White-tailed along large rivers in South Asia to Ayeyarwady basin in Myanmar. Amur breeds across central and eastern Palaearctic and winters throughout Myanmar and continental Southeast Asia. **HABITAT AND HABITS** Favour agricultural land, grassland and scrub in lowlands. Amur winters throughout. White-tailed only found in grassland along large rivers. **STATUS** Locally common resident (White-tailed); common winter visitor (Amur).

White-tailed Stonechat   *Amur Stonechat*   *Amur Stonechat*

Spotted Elachura ■ *Elachura formosa* 10cm

DESCRIPTION Tiny, dark brown and speckled, like small wren or wren-babbler, with short tail. Pale speckling on hindneck and tips of wing-coverts; wings and tail dark rufous

with black bars. Juveniles darker than adults, with heavier speckles. **DISTRIBUTION** Resident in eastern Himalaya, in North and West Myanmar, and into southern China and north Indochina. **HABITAT AND HABITS** Occurs in hilly land, mostly at 500–2,000m, on the ground and in groundcover vegetation within broadleaved evergreen forests. **STATUS** Uncommon resident.

Asian Fairy-bluebird
■ *Irena puella* 25cm

DESCRIPTION In male, most of face, throat and
underparts black; largely black wings; crown, back,
inner wing-coverts, rump, vent and tail-coverts
brilliant glossy sky-blue. Female deep, dark powder-
blue all over; both sexes have reddish eyes and are
quite bulky. **DISTRIBUTION** Resident in South and
Southeast Asia, through Greater Sundas. Throughout
Myanmar. **HABITAT AND HABITS** Found in canopy
and middle storey of evergreen forest and secondary
woodland, extending into hill forests to 1,500m.
Takes many species of fruits and invertebrates, often
snatching food while in flight. Seen singly or in pairs,
except at major fig and other fruit trees, where numbers
can gather. Fine, two-note call, *plip plip*. **STATUS**
Uncommon resident.

Female

Golden-fronted Leafbird ■ *Chloropsis aurifrons* 18–19cm;
Orange-bellied Leafbird ■ *C. hardwickii* 19–21cm

DESCRIPTION Bright sage-green above. Male Golden-fronted has orange forehead and
forecrown, with black mask and yellow band around lower bib and blue shoulder. Female
slightly smaller, with less blue on shoulder. Orange-bellied subtle orange below, with black
sides of face and throat, and long, purplish-black panel along wing. Female grass-green
with orange flush on lower belly and undertail-coverts; limited blue on wing-coverts and
inner secondaries. **DISTRIBUTION** Golden-fronted resident in South and Southeast Asia.
Orange-bellied in foothills of Himalaya, through highlands of
North, West and East Myanmar,
into Southwest China, and
northern Thailand and Lao.
HABITAT AND HABITS Found
in canopy and middle storey
of hilly or montane forests,
and along forested roadsides;
Golden-fronted from lowlands
to 1,550m; Orange-bellied at
roughly 600–2,150m. Male and
female both sing – wide range
of beautiful notes including
imitations of other species.
STATUS Uncommon residents.

Golden-fronted Leafbird

Orange-bellied Leafbird

Orange-bellied Flowerpecker ■ *Dicaeum trigonostigma* 8cm

DESCRIPTION Slaty-blue head, upper breast, back, wings and tail; grey throat; brilliant orange lower breast to vent; orange-yellow lower back and rump. Female olive-grey,

unstreaked, with creamy-yellow rump and centre to belly. **DISTRIBUTION** Resident from Bangladesh, through West, Central, South and Tenasserim, Myanmar, to Peninsular Malaysia, Greater Sundas and the Philippines. **HABITAT AND HABITS** Occurs in edges of lowland evergreen forests upwards to about 900m; occasionally into montane forest edges to 1,500m. Also enters tall plantations, well-wooded parkland, logged forest, and occasionally mangroves. Feeds on various small fruits, including mistletoes, plus insects and nectar. Nest a hanging pouch in understorey. **STATUS** Uncommon resident.

Scarlet-backed Flowerpecker ■ *Dicaeum cruentatum* 9cm

DESCRIPTION Male has scarlet band from forehead and crown down central back and rump; blackish face, breast-sides, scapulars, wings and tail; nearly white from throat

to vent. Female plain light brown, darker on wings and tail, whitish below, with bright scarlet rump. **DISTRIBUTION** Resident from Northeast India, through continental Southeast Asia, to Greater Sundas. Throughout Myanmar. **HABITAT AND HABITS** Occurs in parks, gardens and orchards in lowlands to about 1,200m, open woodland and forest edges. Forages in upper storey, in treetops. **STATUS** Common resident.

Yellow-eared Spiderhunter ■ *Arachnothera chrysogenys* 18cm

DESCRIPTION Dark olive-green with breast and belly faintly streaked, reaching to yellow thighs; bright yellow but often incomplete eye-ring that typically connects with large yellow cheek-patch. Juveniles duller than adults, especially eye-ring and cheek-patch.
DISTRIBUTION Resident in Greater Sundas and extends north along Isthmus of Kra, to far south Tenasserim, Myanmar.
HABITAT AND HABITS Flowers of epiphytes and canopy trees provide most of food, in lowland evergreen rain forests, from sea level upwards; at least visits montane forests to about 1,800m. Also logged forests and tree plantations, and visits roadside trees such as *Erythrina*. **STATUS** Uncommon resident.

Streaked Spiderhunter ■ *Arachnothera magna* 18cm

DESCRIPTION Olive-green above from forehead to tail, and buffy-white below from chin to vent; entire plumage finely streaked blackish; bright orange-yellow feet often clearly visible. **DISTRIBUTION** Resident in eastern Himalaya and Southwest China, through highlands of Southeast Asia. Throughout Myanmar.
HABITAT AND HABITS Characteristic bird of montane forest at around 800–1,800m, in middle and upper storeys, and in roadside vegetation in hills. Takes nectar from banana flowers at forest edges, and insects from tangles of epiphytes and lichen on branches. Quick, single alarm notes and two-note flight call can often be heard.
STATUS Common resident.

Maroon-bellied Sunbird ■ *Leptocoma brasiliana* 10cm

DESCRIPTION Very small. Male entirely dark, from iridescent purple throat to maroon belly, and shining green crown to blue-black back, wings and tail. Female has featureless

brown upperparts, dull yellow underparts, and slightly greyish wash on throat and upper breast. DISTRIBUTION Resident in Southeast Asia and Greater Sundas. West, Central, South and Tenasserim, Myanmar. HABITAT AND HABITS Occurs in lowlands at sea level to 1,200m, from mangroves inland through variety of cultivated land, gardens, secondary forest and forest edges, into broadleaved evergreen forest canopy. STATUS Uncommon resident.

Olive-backed Sunbird ■ *Cynniris jugularis* 12cm

DESCRIPTION Olive-green from crown to rump; lower breast and belly bright deep yellow. In male, forehead, throat and upper breast iridescent blue-black; female overall paler, duller and lacks any blue-black markings. DISTRIBUTION Resident across

Southeast Asia to Australia. Central, South, East and Tenasserim, Myanmar, gradually expanding north in disturbed habitats. HABITAT AND HABITS Locally most common and conspicuous sunbird throughout area, in parks and gardens, scrub, mangroves and plantations. Takes nectar from wide range of flower species and shapes, from mangrove trees to garden flowers, and many invertebrates, especially spiders. Tiny but very active, often in pairs, with territorial males pursuing each other from treetop to treetop. STATUS Common resident.

Black-throated Sunbird ■ *Aethopyga saturata* 11–15cm

DESCRIPTION Male overall very dark, with yellow rump and long central tail feathers; head iridescent blue-black, breast and back maroon, and belly grey. Female olive-grey with pale yellow rump and grey throat. **DISTRIBUTION** Resident in Himalaya into Southwest China. North, West, East and Tenasserim, Myanmar, into highlands of continental Southeast Asia. **HABITAT AND HABITS** Found at 820–2,000m, from canopy to lower storey and forest edges in hills, including stunted forests on ridgetops. Seen singly or in pairs, often in mixed foraging flocks, taking tiny invertebrates, and nectar from tubular flowers of forest epiphytes, as well as from garden flowers and other plants. **STATUS** Common resident.

Green-tailed Sunbird ■ *Aethopyga nipalensis* 12cm

DESCRIPTION Male has iridescent green head sharply defined against yellow underparts, maroon and brown back and wings, bright yellow rump, and green tail with elongated central feathers. Female olive above, slightly greyer on face, yellowish below (brightening towards undertail-coverts), and dark tail with white feather-tips visible below. **DISTRIBUTION** Resident in Himalaya into Southwest China. North, West and East Myanmar, into Thailand and highlands of Indochina. **HABITAT AND HABITS** Occurs mostly in hilly country at 1,400–2750m, lower in winter, in broadleaved evergreen forests, forest edges and associated secondary vegetation. **STATUS** Common resident.

Female

Male

Asian Golden Weaver ■ *Ploceus hypoxanthus* 15cm

DESCRIPTION Particularly heavy billed and sparrow-like. Breeding male bright yellow with black face and chin, blackish-brown wings, tail and upper back with yellowish feather edgings. Female heavily streaked brown and buff on crown, hindneck and back, unmarked warm buff below. **DISTRIBUTION** Resident in continental Southeast Asia and Sumatra. Central and South Myanmar. **HABITAT AND HABITS** Occurs in lowlands in grasses and shrubs close to water (often nests over water), paddy fields and swampy ground. **STATUS** Locally common resident. However, all three weavers are trapped and sold for a pittance outside Buddhist temples. Visitors release the birds for perceived karmic reward.

Adult female

Adult male

Streaked Weaver ■ *Ploceus manyar* 13–14cm

DESCRIPTION Slightly smaller and distinctly less heavy billed than the Asian Golden Weaver (above). In male, yellow confined to crown; rest of plumage heavily streaked, including upper breast. Female similar but no yellow on crown; lighter brown and buff streaking on crown and breast; pale yellow supercilium and chin. **DISTRIBUTION** Resident in South and continental Southeast Asia and Java. North, Central, East and South Myanmar. **HABITAT AND HABITS** Occurs in lowlands to above 900m, in areas dominated by grasses and reeds, with scattered shrubs and trees, often in wetlands. **STATUS** Uncommon resident.

Adult female

Streaked Weaver building a nest

Baya Weaver ■ *Ploceus philippinus* 15cm

DESCRIPTION Chequered brown and blackish back and wings, plain rump and russet-brown breast. In male entire cap deep yellow; ear-coverts and throat dark; minimal streaking on breast. Female has faintly striped brown crown, and buffy-brown throat, face and eyebrow. **DISTRIBUTION** Resident in South and Southeast Asia to Sumatra and Java. Throughout Myanmar. **HABITAT AND HABITS** Found among tall coconut trees, grassland and edges of secondary woodland, where tall grass is adjacent to suitable nesting trees. These are typically acacia, sometimes coconut or bamboo. Several to many males build one to several nests each – a flask of drying grass, cunningly woven, suspended from slender branch. Some are chosen by females for laying eggs. In decline, because nests are poached for sale, plus loss of habitat. **STATUS** Locally common resident.

Red Avadavat ■ *Amandava amandava* 10cm

DESCRIPTION Very small; breeding male deep bright red with dense white spotting below, browner above with pale tips to wing-coverts; may appear nearly black in poor light. Female and non-breeding male greyish-fawn below, brown above, with pale tips to coverts and red rump. Bill and legs pink. **DISTRIBUTION** Resident in South and Southeast Asia to Lesser Sundas. Throughout lowlands of Myanmar. **HABITAT AND HABITS** Occurs in lowlands and hills, occasionally to 1,500m. Rather inconspicuous in small groups in grassland, scrub and agricultural land, on the ground or in low vegetation. **STATUS** Uncommon resident.

White-rumped Munia ■ *Lonchura striata* 12cm

DESCRIPTION Blackish-brown, with crown and back very finely streaked pale; face, upper breast, and uppertail- and lower tail-coverts paler brown; lower breast, belly and rump dirty-white. Tail feathers

slightly pointed. **DISTRIBUTION** Resident in South Asia, through Southeast Asia, to southern China and Taiwan, and south to Sumatra. Throughout Myanmar. **HABITAT AND HABITS** Occurs from lowlands to montane elevations, usually in hilly country, in grassland with scattered woodland, along forest edges and in secondary growth. Seen in small flocks or pairs, taking mostly seeds of various grasses. **STATUS** Common resident.

Scaly-breasted Munia ■ *Lonchura punctulata* 10cm

DESCRIPTION Head, throat, back and wings chestnut, darkest around face; breast and belly white strongly scalloped with black, scallops extending to rump. Juveniles sandy-brown all over like most munias, best identified by association with adults. **DISTRIBUTION** Resident in South and Southeast Asia, into Indonesia and the Philippines. Throughout lowlands of Myanmar, often in hotel gardens. **HABITAT AND HABITS** Associated with human cultivation, especially paddy fields, grassland, old mining land and suburban areas. Eats many types of grass seed, as well as ripening rice, and big flocks can build up. Nest a grassy ball built in dense vegetation, often in ornamental palms. **STATUS** Common resident.

Adult

Juvenile

Chestnut Munia ■ *Lonchura atricapilla* 11cm

DESCRIPTION Entire head and throat black; entire body, wings, and tail bright rufous-chestnut. Bill grey, flushing bright turquoise during breeding. **DISTRIBUTION** Resident in South and Southeast Asia, into Indonesia and the Philippines. Throughout lowlands of Myanmar. **HABITAT AND HABITS** One of the most common munias, in damp grassland, tall, scrubby grass over abandoned land, paddy fields and suburban areas, to maximum of 1,650m. Big flocks can occur in ripe rice, but pairs split off to breed at any time of year. Nest a ball of grass among shrubby plants, or in tall grass, or even in crown of palm tree **STATUS** Locally common resident.

House Sparrow ■ *Passer domesticus* 15cm

DESCRIPTION Male has light grey crown and chestnut brow and nape, separated from black throat by large whitish sides of face; light grey breast, belly and rump; back and wings brown with dark streaking and pale bars. Female light brown with pale supercilium bordered darker; pale grey-buff underparts; brown with dark streaking above; pale wing-bars. **DISTRIBUTION** Across Palearctic, into South and Southeast Asia. Throughout Myanmar and expanding range further east into Indochina. All three *Passer* sparrows found together around temples in Bagan. **HABITAT AND HABITS** Associated with humans, typically in settlements, towns and cities, and in gardens and scrub in lowlands. **STATUS** Common resident.

Plain-backed Sparrow ▪ *Passer flaveolus* 14–15cm

DESCRIPTION Similar to the House Sparrow (p. 147). Male has ashy crown extending all the way down nape; chestnut on either side brighter and paler; smaller black bib

under chin; entire underparts and cheek-patch have yellowish wash. Female has unstreaked, plain upper back, and entire plumage has yellowish wash. **DISTRIBUTION** Resident in driest areas in continental Southeast Asia, including dry zone of North, Central and South and across East Myanmar into Thailand. **HABITAT AND HABITS** Found in dry habitats in lowlands and hills to above 1,500m, from coastal scrub to dry agriculture, reaching into fringes of human settlements but not densely urban areas. **STATUS** Common resident.

Eurasian Tree Sparrow ▪ *Passer montanus* 14cm

DESCRIPTION Chestnut cap and small black bib, separated by grey-white cheeks with black spot on ear-coverts. Back and wing-coverts streaky-brown with black and white streaks and wing-bar; underside buffy-grey. Sexes alike and juveniles merely duller. **DISTRIBUTION** Across Palearctic, through tropical Asia to northern Australia. Throughout Myanmar. **HABITAT AND HABITS** Commonly associated with towns and villages, factories and ports. Often in large flocks, feeding on short-grass areas, on pavements and in roadside bushes. Sometimes does poorly in habitats that are too well managed, especially where nesting opportunities are lost in crevices and roofs of old buildings. Feeds on grass seeds, spilt food and tiny fragments picked from the ground. **STATUS** Common resident. However, all three *Passer* sparrows are trapped and sold for a pittance outside Buddhist temples. Visitors release them for perceived karmic reward.

Paddyfield Pipit ■ *Anthus rufulus* 16cm

DESCRIPTION Fairly slim, upright pipit present all year. Well-spotted breast. Very similar **Richard's Pipit** *A. richardi* bigger, less heavily spotted, typically uttering one-note *shreep*, and present only in winter.

DISTRIBUTION Resident across South and Southeast Asia, into Indonesia and the Philippines. Throughout Myanmar. **HABITAT AND HABITS** Found in short grass areas, dry ground, and cultivation to 1,500m, including airfields and golf courses. Often with wagtails, foraging for small insects including flies and grasshoppers, and spiders. Trots forwards, and draws itself upright on halting, often on tussock or soil clod. Nest well hidden among grass, and very challenging to locate. Typically gives three-note *tcheptcheptchep* flight call when disturbed. **STATUS** Common resident.

Long-billed Pipit ■ *Anthus similis* 20cm

DESCRIPTION Large, lightly streaked, overall rufous-buff pipit. Upper back light brown, indistinctly streaked, wings and tail darker, with buff wing-bars; faint pale supercilium and moustache-streak, and buff underparts. Juveniles scaled above with paler feather edges; more streaked than adults but less rufous-buff below. **DISTRIBUTION** Widespread pockets across Africa, Middle East and South Asia. Easternmost population *A. s. yamethini* in dry zone of North and Central Myanmar. **HABITAT AND HABITS** Found in short grass, dry ground and cultivation to 1,500m, including airfields and golf courses. Often with wagtails, foraging for small insects including flies, grasshoppers and spiders. Trots forward, and draws itself upright on halting, often on tussock or soil clod. Nest well hidden among grass, and very challenging to locate. Typically gives three-note *tcheptcheptchep* flight call when disturbed. **STATUS** Uncommon localized resident.

Grey Wagtail
■ *Motacilla cinerea* 19cm

DESCRIPTION Slim, with long tail bobbed up and down; white outer-tail feathers. Dark grey back, crown and sides of face with white brow; pale yellowish beneath. In flight, white wing-bar and yellow rump visible. **DISTRIBUTION** Widespread in Old World, breeding down to Himalaya and wintering across Southeast Asia and Indonesia. Throughout Myanmar in winter. **HABITAT AND HABITS** Typically seen singly on the ground, on unfrequented roads, logging tracks and especially near streams. Trots after small insects and other invertebrates on soil or rock surfaces, at the water's edge or even on wet tarmac, with tail wagging intermittently. **STATUS** Common winter visitor.

White Wagtail ■ *Motacilla alba* 19cm

DESCRIPTION Variously patterned populations occur. All are slim, lively, tail-wagging birds with some white on forehead, supercilium, sides of face or neck, and lower breast

and belly. Big white panel on bend of wing and coverts; white edges to flight feathers and tail. Upper back light grey to black, and some form of blackish mark on upper breast; in some populations entire throat and upper breast black. In female and non-breeders, black replaced by grey. **DISTRIBUTION** Widespread in Old World, with at least five races breeding in eastern Palearctic and wintering in Southeast Asia. M. *a. alboides* breeds in North Myanmar. **HABITAT AND HABITS** Found in lowlands and to 2,000m, on open ground, often damp, along rivers and at roadsides and in agriculture. **STATUS** Common resident and winter visitor.

Yellow-breasted Greenfinch ■ *Chloris spinoides* 14cm;
Black-headed Greenfinch ■ *C. ambigua* 14cm

DESCRIPTION Greenish-olive above, dark wings with broad yellow bars and pale fringes to flight feathers, and yellow panels at tail-base. Yellow-breasted entirely yellow below, with blackish cheeks outlined by yellow line including supercilium. Black-headed has dark hood, no supercilium and underparts olive-green down to flanks. Females have lighter, streaky heads and some streaking below; heavier in Black-headed. **DISTRIBUTION** Yellow-breasted across Himalaya to North and West Myanmar. Black-headed across Ayeyarwady River in East Myanmar, Southwest China and northern Indochina. **HABITAT AND HABITS** Found at roughly 1,200–2,600m, lower in winter, in flocks, in coniferous and deciduous forest edges, secondary growth and adjacent agricultural land. **STATUS** Locally common residents.

Yellow-breasted Greenfinch

Black-headed Greenfinch

Yellow-breasted Bunting ■ *Emberiza aureola* 15cm;
Little Bunting ■ *E. pusilla* 13cm

DESCRIPTION Streaky brown and sparrow-like. Yellow-breasted has yellow underparts with brown band across upper breast; male with black hood, female streakier. Little Bunting small, short-billed, and streaky all over, except plain pale throat and moustache; when breeding, chestnut sides of face and central crown-stripe. **DISTRIBUTION** Both breed from Scandinavia to Siberia and winter along edge of Himalaya and into lowlands of continental Southeast Asia. Little common winter visitor across North and East Myanmar. Yellow-breasted population has dramatically declined recently, with substantial population still wintering in North, Central, East and South Myanmar. **HABITAT AND HABITS** Yellow-breasted found in lowlands to about 1,400m, wintering on open ground, reeds and agricultural land; Little extends to 2,600m, including secondary growth and forest edges. **STATUS** Respectively, rare and common winter visitors.

Yellow-breasted Bunting

Little Bunting

KEY TO SEASONAL STATUS

BV	Breeding visitor
D	More details needed
I	Introduced
H	Not recorded in past 50 years
P	Passage migrant spring and autumn
R	Resident
R*	Endemic resident
V	Vagrant
WV	Winter visitor

KEY TO GLOBAL THREAT STATUS

CE	Critically Endangered
EN	Endangered
VU	Vulnerable
NT	Near Threatened
LC	Least Concern
DD	Data Deficient

Common Name	Scientific Name	Seasonal Status	Global Threat
Megapodiidae (Megapodes)			
Nicobar Scrubfowl	*Megapodius nicobariensis*	H	VU
Phasianidae (Pheasants, Partridges & Quail)			
Crested Partridge	*Rollulus rouloul*	R	NT
Hill Partridge	*Arborophila torqueola*	R	LC
Rufous-throated Partridge	*Arborophila rufogularis*	R	LC
White-cheeked Partridge	*Arborophila atrogularis*	R	NT
Chestnut-breasted Partridge	*Arborophila mandellii*	R	VU
Bar-backed Partridge	*Arborophila brunneopectus*	R	LC
Green-legged Partridge	*Tropicoperdix chloropus*	R	LC
Chestnut-necklaced Partridge	*Tropicoperdix charltonii*	R	VU
Long-billed Partridge	*Rhizothera longirostris*	R	NT
Ferruginous Partridge	*Caloperdix oculeus*	R	NT
Green Peafowl	*Pavo muticus*	R	EN
Great Argus	*Argusianus argus*	R	NT
Grey Peacock-pheasant	*Polyplectron bicalcaratum*	R	LC
Malayan Peacock Pheasant	*Polyplectron malacense*	R	VU
Common Quail	*Coturnix coturnix*	V	LC
Japanese Quail	*Coturnix japonica*	WV	NT
Rain Quail	*Coturnix coromandelica*	R	LC
Asian Blue Quail	*Synoicus chinensis*	R	LC
Snow Partridge	*Lerwa lerwa*	R	LC
Chinese Francolin	*Francolinus pintadeanus*	R	LC
Mountain Bamboo-partridge	*Bambusicola fytchii*	R	LC
Red Junglefowl	*Gallus gallus*	R	LC
Himalayan Monal	*Lophophorus impejanus*	R	LC
Sclater's Monal	*Lophophorus sclateri*	R	VU
Blyth's Tragopan	*Tragopan blythii*	R	VU
Temminck's Tragopan	*Tragopan temminckii*	R	LC
Blood Pheasant	*Ithaginis cruentus*	R	LC
Mrs Hume's Pheasant	*Syrmaticus humiae*	R	NT
Lady Amherst's Pheasant	*Chrysolophus amherstiae*	R	LC
Common Pheasant	*Phasianus colchicus*	R	LC
Kalij Pheasant	*Lophura leucomelanos*	R	LC
Silver Pheasant	*Lophura nycthemera*	R	LC
Malay Crested Fireback	*Lophura rufa*	R	NT
Siamese Fireback	*Lophura diardi*	R	LC
Anatidae (Ducks, Geese & Swans)			
Fulvous Whistling-duck	*Dendrocygna bicolor*	R	LC
Lesser Whistling-duck	*Dendrocygna javanica*	R	LC
Bar-headed Goose	*Anser indicus*	WV	LC
Greylag Goose	*Anser anser*	WV	LC
Bean Goose	*Anser fabalis*	V	LC
Greater White-fronted Goose	*Anser albifrons*	WV	LC

Common Name	Scientific Name	Seasonal Status	Global Threat
Lesser White-fronted Goose	Anser erythropus	V	VU
Common Goldeneye	Bucephala clangula	WV	LC
Smew	Mergellus albellus	WV	LC
Goosander	Mergus merganser	WV	LC
Scaly-sided Merganser	Mergus squamatus	V	EN
Red-breasted Merganser	Mergus serrator	V	LC
Common Shelduck	Tadorna tadorna	WV	LC
Ruddy Shelduck	Tadorna ferruginea	WV	LC
Knob-billed Duck	Sarkidiornis melanotos	R	LC
Cotton Pygmy-goose	Nettapus coromandelianus	R	LC
Mandarin Duck	Aix galericulata	WV	LC
White-winged Duck	Asarcornis scutulata	R	EN
Red-crested Pochard	Netta rufina	WV	LC
Common Pochard	Aythya ferina	WV	VU
Baer's Pochard	Aythya baeri	WV	CR
Ferruginous Duck	Aythya nyroca	WV	NT
Tufted Duck	Aythya fuligula	WV	LC
Greater Scaup	Aythya marila	WV	LC
Pink-headed Duck	Rhodonessa caryophyllacea	H	CR
Garganey	Spatula querquedula	WV	LC
Northern Shoveler	Spatula clypeata	WV	LC
Baikal Teal	Sibirionetta formosa	WV	LC
Falcated Duck	Mareca falcata	WV	NT
Gadwall	Mareca strepera	WV	LC
Eurasian Wigeon	Mareca penelope	WV	LC
Indian Spot-billed Duck	Anas poecilorhyncha	R	LC
Chinese Spot-billed Duck	Anas zonorhyncha	WV	LC
Mallard	Anas platyrhynchos	WV	LC
Andaman Teal	Anas albogularis	R	VU
Northern Pintail	Anas acuta	WV	LC
Common Teal	Anas crecca	WV	LC
Podicipedidae (Grebes)			
Little Grebe	Tachybaptus ruficollis	R	LC
Great Crested Grebe	Podiceps cristatus	WV	LC
Horned Grebe	Podiceps auritus	V	VU
Black-necked Grebe	Podiceps nigricollis	WV	LC
Phaethontidae (Tropicbirds)			
Red-billed Tropicbird	Phaethon aethereus	V	LC
White-tailed Tropicbird	Phaethon lepturus	V	LC
Columbidae (Pigeons & Doves)			
Rock Dove	Columba livia	I	LC
Snow Pigeon	Columba leuconota	R	LC
Speckled Woodpigeon	Columba hodgsonii	R	LC
Ashy Woodpigeon	Columba pulchricollis	R	LC
Pale-capped Pigeon	Columba punicea	R	VU
Oriental Turtle-dove	Streptopelia orientalis	R	LC
Burmese Collared-dove	Streptopelia xanthocycla	R*	LC
Red Turtle-dove	Streptopelia tranquebarica	R	LC
Eastern Spotted Dove	Spilopelia chinensis	R	LC
Barred Cuckoo-dove	Macropygia unchall	R	LC
Little Cuckoo-dove	Macropygia ruficeps	R	LC
Zebra Dove	Geopelia striata	R	LC
Nicobar Pigeon	Caloenas nicobarica	R	NT
Asian Emerald Dove	Chalcophaps indica	R	LC
Cinnamon-headed Green-pigeon	Treron fulvicollis	R	NT
Pink-necked Green-pigeon	Treron vernans	R	LC
Orange-breasted Green-pigeon	Treron bicinctus	R	LC
Ashy-headed Green-pigeon	Treron phayrei	R	NT
Andaman Green-pigeon	Treron chloropterus	R	NT
Thick-billed Green-pigeon	Treron curvirostra	R	LC
Large Green-pigeon	Treron capellei	R	VU
Yellow-footed Green-pigeon	Treron phoenicopterus	R	LC
Pin-tailed Green-pigeon	Treron apicauda	R	LC
Wedge-tailed Green-pigeon	Treron sphenurus	R	LC
Green Imperial-pigeon	Ducula aenea	R	LC

Common Name	Scientific Name	Seasonal Status	Global Threat
Mountain Imperial-pigeon	Ducula badia	R	LC
Pied Imperial-pigeon	Ducula bicolor	R	LC
Jambu Fruit-dove	Ramphiculus jambu	V	NT
Podargidae (Frogmouths)			
Hodgson's Frogmouth	Batrachostomus hodgsoni	R	LC
Blyth's Frogmouth	Batrachostomus affinis	R	LC
Caprimulgidae (Nightjars)			
Great Eared-nightjar	Lyncornis macrotis	R	LC
Grey Nightjar	Caprimulgus jotaka	R	LC
Large-tailed Nightjar	Caprimulgus macrurus	R	LC
Indian Nightjar	Caprimulgus asiaticus	R	LC
Savanna Nightjar	Caprimulgus affinis	R	LC
Hemiprocnidae (Treeswifts)			
Crested Treeswift	Hemiprocne coronata	R	LC
Grey-rumped Treeswift	Hemiprocne longipennis	R	LC
Whiskered Treeswift	Hemiprocne comata	R	LC
Apodidae (Swifts)			
Silver-rumped Spinetail	Rhaphidura leucopygialis	R	LC
White-throated Needletail	Hirundapus caudacutus	R	LC
Silver-backed Needletail	Hirundapus cochinchinensis	R	LC
Brown-backed Needletail	Hirundapus giganteus	R	LC
Plume-toed Swiftlet	Collocalia affinis	R	LC
Himalayan Swiftlet	Aerodramus brevirostris	R	LC
Black-nest Swiftlet	Aerodramus maximus	R	LC
Germain's Swiftlet	Aerodramus germani	R	LC
Asian Palm-swift	Cypsiurus balasiensis	R	LC
Alpine Swift	Tachymarptis melba	V	LC
Cook's Swift	Apus cooki	R	LC
Dark-rumped Swift	Apus acuticauda	R	VU
Pacific Swift	Apus pacificus	R	LC
House Swift	Apus nipalensis	R	LC
Cuculidae (Cuckoos)			
Greater Coucal	Centropus sinenses	R	LC
Andaman Coucal	Centropus andamanensis	R	LC
Lesser Coucal	Centropus bengalensis	R	LC
Raffles's Malkoha	Rhinortha chlorophaea	R	LC
Red-billed Malkoha	Zanclostomus javanicus	R	LC
Black-bellied Malkoha	Phaenicophaeus diardi	R	NT
Chestnut-bellied Malkoha	Phaenicophaeus sumatranus	R	NT
Green-billed Malkoha	Phaenicophaeus tristis	R	LC
Chestnut-breasted Malkoha	Phaenicophaeus curvirostris	R	LC
Pied Cuckoo	Clamator jacobinus	R	LC
Chestnut-winged Cuckoo	Clamator coromandus	R	LC
Asian Koel	Eudynamys scolopaceus	R	LC
Asian Emerald Cuckoo	Chrysococcyx maculatus	R	LC
Violet Cuckoo	Chrysococcyx xanthorhynchus	R	LC
Banded Bay Cuckoo	Cacomantis sonneratii	R	LC
Plaintive Cuckoo	Cacomantis merulinus	R	LC
Grey-bellied Cuckoo	Cacomantis passerinus	V	LC
Brush Cuckoo	Cacomantis variolosus	R	LC
Square-tailed Drongo-cuckoo	Surniculus lugubris	R	LC
Large Hawk-cuckoo	Hierococcyx sparverioides	R	LC
Common Hawk-cuckoo	Hierococcyx varius	R	LC
Moustached Hawk-cuckoo	Hierococcyx vagans	R	NT
Whistling Hawk-cuckoo	Hierococcyx nisicolor	R	LC
Malay Hawk-cuckoo	Hierococcyx fugax	R	LC
Indian Cuckoo	Cuculus micropterus	R	LC
Common Cuckoo	Cuculus canorus	BV	LC
Oriental Cuckoo	Cuculus saturatus	BV	LC
Lesser Cuckoo	Cuculus poliocephalus	BV	LC
Heliornithidae (Finfoots)			
Masked Finfoot	Heliopais personatus	R	EN
Rallidae (Rails, Crakes & Coots)			
Red-legged Crake	Rallina fasciata	R	LC
Slaty-legged Crake	Rallina eurizonoides	R	LC

Common Name	Scientific Name	Seasonal Status	Global Threat
Brown-cheeked Rail	Rallus indicus	WV	LC
Slaty-breasted Rail	Lewinia striata	R	LC
Spotted Crake	Porzana porzana	V	LC
Ruddy-breasted Crake	Zapornia fusca	R	LC
Brown Crake	Zapornia akool	R	LC
Baillon's Crake	Zapornia pusilla	R	LC
Black-tailed Crake	Zapornia bicolor	R	LC
White-breasted Waterhen	Amaurornis phoenicurus	R	LC
White-browed Crake	Amaurornis cinerea	R	LC
Watercock	Gallicrex cinerea	R	LC
Grey-headed Swamphen	Porphyrio poliocephalus	R	LC
Common Moorhen	Gallinula chloropus	R	LC
Common Coot	Fulica atra	R	LC
Gruidae (Cranes)			
Sarus Crane	Antigone antigone	R	VU
Demoiselle Crane	Anthropoides virgo	V	LC
Common Crane	Grus grus	WV	LC
Otididae (Bustards)			
Great Bustard	Otis tarda	H	VU
Gaviidae (Loons)			
Yellow-billed Loon	Gavia adamsii	V	NT
Oceanitidae (Southern Storm-petrels)			
Wilson's Storm-petrel	Oceanites oceanicus	V	LC
Procellariidae (Petrels & Shearwaters)			
Short-tailed Shearwater	Ardenna tenuirostris	V	LC
Jouanin's Petrel	Bulweria fallax	V	NT
Ciconiidae (Storks)			
Greater Adjutant	Leptoptilos dubius	R	EN
Lesser Adjutant	Leptoptilos javanicus	R	VU
Painted Stork	Mycteria leucocephala	R	NT
Asian Openbill	Anastomus oscitans	R	LC
Black Stork	Ciconia nigra	WV	LC
Asian Woollyneck	Ciconia episcopus	R	VU
Storm's Stork	Ciconia stormi	R	EN
White Stork	Ciconia ciconia	V	LC
Black-necked Stork	Ephippiorhynchus asiaticus	R	NT
Threskiornithidae (Ibises & Spoonbills)			
Eurasian Spoonbill	Platalea leucorodia	WV	LC
Black-headed Ibis	Threskiornis melanocephalus	R	NT
White-shouldered Ibis	Pseudibis davisoni	H	CR
Red-naped Ibis	Pseudibis papillosa	H	LC
Glossy Ibis	Plegadis falcinellus	R	LC
Ardeidae (Herons, Egrets & Bitterns)			
Eurasian Bittern	Botaurus stellaris	WV	LC
Yellow Bittern	Ixobrychus sinensis	R	LC
Schrenck's Bittern	Ixobrychus eurhythmus	P	LC
Cinnamon Bittern	Ixobrychus cinnamomeus	R	LC
Black Bittern	Ixobrychus flavicollis	R	LC
Malay Night-heron	Gorsachius melanolophus	R	LC
Black-crowned Night-heron	Nycticorax nycticorax	R	LC
Green-backed Heron	Butorides striata	R	LC
Indian Pond-heron	Ardeola grayii	R	LC
Chinese Pond-heron	Ardeola bacchus	R	LC
Javan Pond-heron	Ardeola speciosa	R	LC
Cattle Egret	Bubulcus ibis	R	LC
Grey Heron	Ardea cinerea	R	LC
White-bellied Heron	Ardea insignis	R	CR
Great-billed Heron	Ardea sumatrana	R	LC
Goliath Heron	Ardea goliath	H	LC
Purple Heron	Ardea purpurea	R	LC
Great White Egret	Ardea alba	R	LC
Intermediate Egret	Ardea intermedia	R	LC
Little Egret	Egretta garzetta	R	LC
Pacific Reef-egret	Egretta sacra	R	LC
Chinese Egret	Egretta eulophotes	WV	VU

Common Name	Scientific Name	Seasonal Status	Global Threat
Pelecanidae (Pelicans)			
Spot-billed Pelican	*Pelecanus philippensis*	R	NT
Great White Pelican	*Pelecanus onocrotalus*	V	LC
Fregatidae (Frigatebirds)			
Great Frigatebird	*Fregata minor*	V	LC
Sulidae (Gannets & Boobies)			
Brown Booby	*Sula leucogaster*	V	LC
Red-footed Booby	*Sula sula*	V	LC
Phalacrocoracidae (Cormorants)			
Little Cormorant	*Microcarbo niger*	R	LC
Great Cormorant	*Phalacrocorax carbo*	R	LC
Indian Cormorant	*Phalacrocorax fuscicollis*	R	LC
Anhingidae (Darters)			
Oriental Darter	*Anhinga melanogaster*	R	NT
Burhinidae (Thick-knees)			
Indian Thick-knee	*Burhinus indicus*	R	LC
Great Thick-knee	*Esacus recurvirostris*	R	NT
Beach Thick-knee	*Esacus magnirostris*	R	NT
Haematopodidae (Oystercatchers)			
Eurasian Oystercatcher	*Haematopus ostralegus*	WV	NT
Ibidorhynchidae (Ibisbill)			
Ibisbill	*Ibidorhyncha struthersii*	WV	LC
Recurvirostridae (Avocets & Stilts)			
Pied Avocet	*Recurvirostra avosetta*	WV	LC
Black-winged Stilt	*Himantopus himantopus*	R	LC
Charadriidae (Plovers)			
Grey Plover	*Pluvialis squatarola*	WV	LC
Pacific Golden Plover	*Pluvialis fulva*	WV	LC
Common Ringed Plover	*Charadrius hiaticula*	WV	LC
Long-billed Plover	*Charadrius placidus*	WV	LC
Little Ringed Plover	*Charadrius dubius*	R	LC
Kentish Plover	*Charadrius alexandrinus*	WV	LC
White-faced Plover	*Charadrius dealbatus*	WV	DD
Malay Plover	*Charadrius peronii*	R	NT
Lesser Sandplover	*Charadrius mongolus*	WV	LC
Greater Sandplover	*Charadrius leschenaultii*	WV	LC
Northern Lapwing	*Vanellus vanellus*	WV	NT
River Lapwing	*Vanellus duvaucelii*	R	NT
Yellow-wattled Lapwing	*Vanellus malabaricus*	V	LC
Grey-headed Lapwing	*Vanellus cinereus*	WV	LC
Red-wattled Lapwing	*Vanellus indicus*	R	LC
Rostratulidae (Painted-snipes)			
Greater Painted-snipe	*Rostratula benghalensis*	R	LC
Jacanidae (Jacanas)			
Pheasant-tailed Jacana	*Hydrophasianus chirurgus*	R	LC
Bronze-winged Jacana	*Metopidius indicus*	R	LC
Scolopacidae (Sandpipers, Snipe & Phalaropes)			
Red-necked Phalarope	*Phalaropus lobatus*	V	LC
Whimbrel	*Numenius phaeopus*	WV	LC
Eurasian Curlew	*Numenius arquata*	WV	NT
Far Eastern Curlew	*Numenius madagascariensis*	WV	EN
Bar-tailed Godwit	*Limosa lapponica*	WV	NT
Black-tailed Godwit	*Limosa limosa*	WV	NT
Ruddy Turnstone	*Arenaria interpres*	WV	LC
Great Knot	*Calidris tenuirostris*	WV	EN
Red Knot	*Calidris canutus*	WV	NT
Ruff	*Calidris pugnax*	WV	LC
Broad-billed Sandpiper	*Calidris falcinellus*	WV	LC
Sharp-tailed Sandpiper	*Calidris acuminata*	WV	LC
Curlew Sandpiper	*Calidris ferruginea*	WV	NT
Temminck's Stint	*Calidris temminckii*	WV	LC
Long-toed Stint	*Calidris subminuta*	WV	LC
Spoon-billed Sandpiper	*Calidris pygmaea*	WV	CR
Red-necked Stint	*Calidris ruficollis*	WV	NT
Sanderling	*Calidris alba*	WV	LC

Common Name	Scientific Name	Seasonal Status	Global Threat
Dunlin	Calidris alpina	WV	LC
Little Stint	Calidris minuta	WV	LC
Asian Dowitcher	Limnodromus semipalmatus	WV	NT
Eurasian Woodcock	Scolopax rusticola	WV	LC
Solitary Snipe	Gallinago solitaria	WV	LC
Wood Snipe	Gallinago nemoricola	R	VU
Pintail Snipe	Gallinago stenura	WV	LC
Swinhoe's Snipe	Gallinago megala	WV	LC
Great Snipe	Gallinago media	V	NT
Common Snipe	Gallinago gallinago	WV	LC
Jack Snipe	Lymnocryptes minimus	WV	LC
Terek Sandpiper	Xenus cinereus	WV	LC
Common Sandpiper	Actitis hypoleucos	WV	LC
Green Sandpiper	Tringa ochropus	WV	LC
Gray-tailed Tattler	Tringa brevipes	WV	NT
Spotted Redshank	Tringa erythropus	WV	LC
Common Greenshank	Tringa nebularia	WV	LC
Common Redshank	Tringa totanus	WV	LC
Wood Sandpiper	Tringa glareola	WV	LC
Marsh Sandpiper	Tringa stagnatilis	WV	LC
Spotted Greenshank	Tringa guttifer	WV	EN
Turnicidae (Buttonquails)			
Common Buttonquail	Turnix sylvaticus	R	LC
Yellow-legged Buttonquail	Turnix tanki	R	LC
Barred Buttonquail	Turnix suscitator	R	LC
Dromadidae (Crab-plover)			
Crab-plover	Dromas ardeola	WV	LC
Glareolidae (Courser & Pratincoles)			
Oriental Pratincole	Glareola maldivarum	BV	LC
Small Pratincole	Glareola lactea	R	LC
Laridae (Gulls, Terns & Skimmers)			
Brown Noddy	Anous stolidus	V	LC
Indian Skimmer	Rynchops albicollis	R	VU
Sabine's Gull	Xema sabini	V	LC
Black-legged Kittiwake	Rissa tridactyla	WV	VU
Slender-billed Gull	Larus genei	WV	LC
Brown-headed Gull	Larus brunnicephalus	WV	LC
Black-headed Gull	Larus ridibundus	WV	LC
Pallas's Gull	Larus ichthyaetus	WV	LC
Lesser Black-backed Gull	Larus fuscus	WV	LC
Sooty Tern	Onychoprion fuscatus	V	LC
Bridled Tern	Onychoprion anaethetus	V	LC
Little Tern	Sternula albifrons	R	LC
Gull-billed Tern	Gelochelidon nilotica	WV	LC
Caspian Tern	Hydroprogne caspia	WV	LC
Whiskered Tern	Chlidonias hybrida	WV	LC
White-winged Tern	Chlidonias leucopterus	WV	LC
Black Tern	Chlidonias niger	WV	LC
River Tern	Sterna aurantia	R	NT
Roseate Tern	Sterna dougallii	R	LC
Black-naped Tern	Sterna sumatrana	WV	LC
Common Tern	Sterna hirundo	WV	LC
Black-bellied Tern	Sterna acuticauda	R	EN
Lesser Crested Tern	Thalasseus bengalensis	WV	LC
Greater Crested Tern	Thalasseus bergii	R	LC
Stercorariidae (Skuas)			
Pomarine Jaeger	Stercorarius pomarinus	WV	LC
Tytonidae (Barn-owls)			
Oriental Bay-owl	Phodilus badius	R	LC
Australasian Grass-owl	Tyto longimembris	R	LC
Barn Owl	Tyto alba	R	LC
Strigidae (Typical Owls)			
Brown Boobook	Ninox scutulata	R	LC
Collared Owlet	Glaucidium brodiei	R	LC
Asian Barred Owlet	Glaucidium cuculoides	R	LC
Jungle Owlet	Glaucidium radiatum	D	LC

Common Name	Scientific Name	Seasonal Status	Global Threat
Spotted Owlet	*Athene brama*	R	LC
White-fronted Scops-owl	*Otus sagittatus*	R	VU
Collared Scops-owl	*Otus lettia*	R	LC
Mountain Scops-owl	*Otus spilocephalus*	R	LC
Oriental Scops-owl	*Otus sunia*	R	LC
Short-eared Owl	*Asio flammeus*	WV	LC
Spotted Wood-owl	*Strix seloputo*	R	LC
Brown Wood-owl	*Strix leptogrammica*	R	LC
Himalayan Owl	*Strix nivicolum*	R	LC
Barred Eagle-owl	*Bubo sumatranus*	R	LC
Spot-bellied Eagle-owl	*Bubo nipalensis*	R	LC
Dusky Eagle-owl	*Bubo coromandus*	R	LC
Brown Fish-owl	*Ketupa zeylonensis*	R	LC
Tawny Fish-owl	*Ketupa flavipes*	R	LC
Buffy Fish-owl	*Ketupa ketupu*	R	LC
Pandionidae (Osprey)			
Osprey	*Pandion haliaetus*	WV	LC
Accipitridae (Hawks & Eagles)			
Black-winged Kite	*Elanus caeruleus*	R	LC
Oriental Honey-buzzard	*Pernis ptilorhynchus*	R	LC
Jerdon's Baza	*Aviceda jerdoni*	R	LC
Black Baza	*Aviceda leuphotes*	R	LC
Egyptian Vulture	*Neophron percnopterus*	V	EN
Crested Serpent-eagle	*Spilornis cheela*	R	LC
Short-toed Snake-eagle	*Circaetus gallicus*	WV	LC
Red-headed Vulture	*Sarcogyps calvus*	R	CR
Himalayan Griffon	*Gyps himalayensis*	WV	NT
White-rumped Vulture	*Gyps bengalensis*	R	CR
Slender-billed Vulture	*Gyps tenuirostris*	R	CR
Cinereous Vulture	*Aegypius monachus*	WV	NT
Bat Hawk	*Macheiramphus alcinus*	R	LC
Mountain Hawk-eagle	*Nisaetus nipalensis*	R	LC
Wallace's Hawk-eagle	*Nisaetus nanus*	R	VU
Changeable Hawk-eagle	*Nisaetus cirrhatus*	R	LC
Rufous-bellied Eagle	*Lophotriorchis kienerii*	R	NT
Black Eagle	*Ictinaetus malaiensis*	R	LC
Indian Spotted Eagle	*Clanga hastata*	R	VU
Greater Spotted Eagle	*Clanga clanga*	WV	VU
Tawny Eagle	*Aquila rapax*	V	VU
Steppe Eagle	*Aquila nipalensis*	WV	EN
Eastern Imperial Eagle	*Aquila heliaca*	WV	VU
Bonelli's Eagle	*Aquila fasciata*	R	LC
Booted Eagle	*Hieraaetus pennatus*	WV	LC
Western Marsh-harrier	*Circus aeruginosus*	WV	LC
Eastern Marsh-harrier	*Circus spilonotus*	WV	LC
Hen Harrier	*Circus cyaneus*	WV	LC
Pallid Harrier	*Circus macrourus*	WV	NT
Pied Harrier	*Circus melanoleucos*	WV	LC
Montagu's Harrier	*Circus pygargus*	WV	LC
Crested Goshawk	*Accipiter trivirgatus*	R	LC
Shikra	*Accipiter badius*	R	LC
Chinese Sparrowhawk	*Accipiter soloensis*	P	LC
Japanese Sparrowhawk	*Accipiter gularis*	P	LC
Besra	*Accipiter virgatus*	R	LC
Eurasian Sparrowhawk	*Accipiter nisus*	R	LC
Northern Goshawk	*Accipiter gentilis*	R	LC
White-bellied Sea-eagle	*Haliaeetus leucogaster*	R	LC
Pallas's Fish-eagle	*Haliaeetus leucoryphus*	R	EN
White-tailed Sea-eagle	*Haliaeetus albicilla*	WV	LC
Lesser Fish-eagle	*Icthyophaga humilis*	R	NT
Grey-headed Fish-eagle	*Icthyophaga ichthyaetus*	R	NT
Brahminy Kite	*Haliastur indus*	R	LC
Black Kite	*Milvus govinda*	R	LC
Black-eared Kite	*Milvus migrans*	R	LC
White-eyed Buzzard	*Butastur teesa*	R	LC

Common Name	Scientific Name	Seasonal Status	Global Threat
Rufous-winged Buzzard	*Butastur liventer*	R	LC
Grey-faced Buzzard	*Butastur indicus*	WV	LC
Japanese Buzzard	*Buteo japonicus*	WV	LC
Himalayan Buzzard	*Buteo refectus*	R	LC
Long-legged Buzzard	*Buteo rufinus*	WV	LC
Trogonidae (Trogons)			
Orange-breasted Trogon	*Harpactes oreskios*	R	LC
Scarlet-rumped Trogon	*Harpactes duvaucelii*	R	NT
Red-headed Trogon	*Harpactes erythrocephalus*	R	LC
Ward's Trogon	*Harpactes wardi*	R	NT
Bucerotidae (Hornbills)			
White-crowned Hornbill	*Berenicornis comatus*	R	EN
Helmeted Hornbill	*Rhinoplax vigil*	R	CR
Great Hornbill	*Buceros bicornis*	R	VU
Bushy-crested Hornbill	*Anorrhinus galeritus*	R	NT
Austen's Brown Hornbill	*Anorrhinus austeni*	R	NT
Tickell's Brown Hornbill	*Anorrhinus tickelli*	R	NT
Black Hornbill	*Anthracoceros malayanus*	R	VU
Oriental Pied Hornbill	*Anthracoceros albirostris*	R	LC
Rufous-necked Hornbill	*Aceros nipalensis*	R	VU
Wreathed Hornbill	*Rhyticeros undulatus*	R	VU
Plain-pouched Hornbill	*Rhyticeros subruficollis*	R	VU
Upupidae (Hoopoes)			
Eurasian Hoopoe	*Upupa epops*	R	LC
Meropidae (Bee-eaters)			
Red-bearded Bee-eater	*Nyctyornis amictus*	R	LC
Blue-bearded Bee-eater	*Nyctyornis athertoni*	R	LC
Asian Green Bee-eater	*Merops orientalis*	R	LC
Chestnut-headed Bee-eater	*Merops leschenaulti*	R	LC
Blue-throated Bee-eater	*Merops viridis*	R	LC
Blue-tailed Bee-eater	*Merops philippinus*	R	LC
Coraciidae (Rollers)			
Indochinese Roller	*Coracias affinis*	R	LC
Oriental Dollarbird	*Eurystomus orientalis*	R	LC
Alcedinidae (Kingfishers)			
Oriental Dwarf-kingfisher	*Ceyx erithaca*	R	LC
Malay Blue-banded Kingfisher	*Alcedo peninsulae*	R	NT
Blue-eared Kingfisher	*Alcedo meninting*	R	LC
Blyth's Kingfisher	*Alcedo hercules*	R	NT
Common Kingfisher	*Alcedo atthis*	R	LC
Crested Kingfisher	*Megaceryle lugubris*	R	LC
Pied Kingfisher	*Ceryle rudis*	R	LC
Banded Kingfisher	*Lacedo pulchella*	R	LC
Stork-billed Kingfisher	*Pelargopsis capensis*	R	LC
Brown-winged Kingfisher	*Pelargopsis amauroptera*	R	NT
Ruddy Kingfisher	*Halcyon coromanda*	R	LC
White-breasted Kingfisher	*Halcyon smyrnensis*	R	LC
Black-capped Kingfisher	*Halcyon pileata*	WV	LC
Rufous-collared Kingfisher	*Actenoides concretus*	R	NT
Collared Kingfisher	*Todiramphus chloris*	R	LC
Megalaimidae (Asian Barbets)			
Sooty Barbet	*Caloramphus hayii*	R	NT
Coppersmith Barbet	*Psilopogon haemacephalus*	R	LC
Blue-eared Barbet	*Psilopogon cyanotis*	R	LC
Great Barbet	*Psilopogon virens*	R	LC
Red-throated Barbet	*Psilopogon mystacophanos*	R	NT
Red-crowned Barbet	*Psilopogon rafflesii*	R	NT
Lineated Barbet	*Psilopogon lineatus*	R	LC
Golden-throated Barbet	*Psilopogon franklinii*	R	LC
Gold-whiskered Barbet	*Psilopogon chrysopogon*	R	LC
Moustached Barbet	*Psilopogon incognitus*	R	LC
Blue-throated Barbet	*Psilopogon asiaticus*	R	LC
Indicatoridae (Honeyguides)			
Yellow-rumped Honeyguide	*Indicator xanthonotus*	R	NT
Malay Honeyguide	*Indicator archipelagicus*	R	NT

Common Name	Scientific Name	Seasonal Status	Global Threat
Picidae (Woodpeckers)			
Eurasian Wryneck	Jynx torquilla	WV	LC
Rufous Piculet	Sasia abnormis	R	LC
White-browed Piculet	Sasia ochracea	R	LC
Speckled Piculet	Picumnus innominatus	R	LC
Grey-and-buff Woodpecker	Hemicircus sordidus	R	LC
Heart-spotted Woodpecker	Hemicircus canente	R	LC
Maroon Woodpecker	Blythipicus rubiginosus	R	LC
Bay Woodpecker	Blythipicus pyrrhotis	R	LC
Greater Flameback	Chrysocolaptes guttacristatus	R	LC
Olive-backed Woodpecker	Dinopium rafflesii	R	NT
Himalayan Flameback	Dinopium shorii	R	LC
Common Flameback	Dinopium javanense	R	LC
Black-Rumped Flameback	Dinopium benghalense	R	LC
Pale-headed Woodpecker	Gecinulus grantia	R	LC
Bamboo Woodpecker	Gecinulus viridis	R	LC
Rufous Woodpecker	Micropternus brachyurus	R	LC
Buff-rumped Woodpecker	Meiglyptes grammithorax	R	LC
Black-and-buff Woodpecker	Meiglyptes jugularis	R	LC
Buff-necked Woodpecker	Meiglyptes tukki	R	NT
Banded Woodpecker	Chrysophlegma miniaceum	R	LC
Chequer-throated Yellownape	Chrysophlegma humii	R	NT
Greater Yellownape	Chrysophlegma flavinucha	R	LC
Crimson-winged Woodpecker	Picus puniceus	R	LC
Lesser Yellownape	Picus chlorolophus	R	LC
Streak-throated Woodpecker	Picus xanthopygaeus	R	LC
Laced Woodpecker	Picus vittatus	R	LC
Streak-breasted Woodpecker	Picus viridanus	R	LC
Black-naped Woodpecker	Picus guerini	R	LC
Black-headed Woodpecker	Picus erythropygius	R	LC
Great Slaty Woodpecker	Mulleripicus pulverulentus	R	VU
White-bellied Woodpecker	Dryocopus javensis	R	LC
Grey-capped Woodpecker	Picoides canicapillus	R	LC
Yellow-crowned Woodpecker	Leiopicus mahrattensis	R	LC
Scarlet-breasted Woodpecker	Dryobates cathpharius	R	LC
Crimson-breasted Woodpecker	Dryobates pernyii	R	LC
Rufous-bellied Woodpecker	Dendrocopos hyperythrus	R	LC
Stripe-breasted Woodpecker	Dendrocopos atratus	R	LC
Fulvous-breasted Woodpecker	Dendrocopos macei	R	LC
Freckle-breasted Woodpecker	Dendrocopos analis	R	LC
Darjeeling Woodpecker	Dendrocopos darjellensis	R	LC
Great Spotted Woodpecker	Dendrocopos major	R	LC
Falconidae (Falcons & Caracaras)			
Pied Falconet	Microhierax melanoleucos	R	LC
Collared Falconet	Microhierax caerulescens	R	LC
Black-thighed Falconet	Microhierax fringillarius	R	LC
White-rumped Pygmy-falcon	Polihierax insignis	R	NT
Lesser Kestrel	Falco naumanni	WV	LC
Common Kestrel	Falco tinnunculus	R	LC
Amur Falcon	Falco amurensis	P	LC
Merlin	Falco columbarius	V	LC
Eurasian Hobby	Falco subbuteo	P	LC
Oriental Hobby	Falco severus	R	LC
Laggar Falcon	Falco jugger	R	NT
Peregrine Falcon	Falco peregrinus	R	LC
Psittacidae (Parrots)			
Vernal Hanging-parrot	Loriculus vernalis	R	LC
Blue-crowned Hanging-parrot	Loriculus galgulus	R	LC
Blue-rumped Parrot	Psittinus cyanurus	R	NT
Grey-headed Parakeet	Psittacula finschii	R	NT
Blossom-headed Parakeet	Psittacula roseata	R	NT
Red-breasted Parakeet	Psittacula alexandri	R	NT
Long-tailed Parakeet	Psittacula longicauda	R	VU
Alexandrine Parakeet	Psittacula eupatria	R	NT
Rose-ringed Parakeet	Psittacula krameri	R	LC

Common Name	Scientific Name	Seasonal Status	Global Threat
Pittidae (Pittas)			
Garnet Pitta	Erythropitta granatina	R	NT
Eared Pitta	Hydrornis phayrei	R	LC
Rusty-naped Pitta	Hydrornis oatesi	R	LC
Blue-naped Pitta	Hydrornis nipalensis	R	LC
Giant Pitta	Hydrornis caeruleus	R	NT
Blue Pitta	Hydrornis cyaneus	R	LC
Gurney's Pitta	Hydrornis gurneyi	R*	CR
Blue-winged Pitta	Pitta moluccensis	BV	LC
Mangrove Pitta	Pitta megarhyncha	R	NT
Hooded Pitta	Pitta sordida	BV	LC
Eurylaimidae (Typical Broadbills)			
Long-tailed Broadbill	Psarisomus dalhousiae	R	LC
Dusky Broadbill	Corydon sumatranus	R	LC
Black-and-red Broadbill	Cymbirhynchus macrorhynchos	R	LC
Irrawaddy Broadbill	Cymbirhynchus affinis	R*	DD
Silver-breasted Broadbill	Serilophus lunatus	R	LC
Grey-browed Broadbill	Serilophus rubropygius	R	LC
Banded Broadbill	Eurylaimus harterti	R	LC
Black-and-yellow Broadbill	Eurylaimus ochromalus	R	NT
Calyptomenidae (African & Green Broadbills)			
Green Broadbill	Calyptomena viridis	R	NT
Acanthizidae (Thornbills)			
Golden-bellied Gerygone	Gerygone sulphurea	R	LC
Oriolidae (Old World Orioles)			
Dark-throated Oriole	Oriolus xanthonotus	R	NT
Maroon Oriole	Oriolus traillii	R	LC
Black-hooded Oriole	Oriolus xanthornus	R	LC
Black-naped Oriole	Oriolus chinensis	R	LC
Slender-billed Oriole	Oriolus tenuirostris	R	LC
Pachycephalidae (Whistlers)			
Mangrove Whistler	Pachycephala cinerea	R	LC
Vireonidae (Vireos)			
Black-headed Shrike-babbler	Pteruthius rufiventer	R	LC
Blyth's Shrike-babbler	Pteruthius aeralatus	R	LC
Green Shrike-babbler	Pteruthius xanthochlorus	R	LC
Black-eared Shrike-babbler	Pteruthius melanotis	R	LC
Trilling Shrike-babbler	Pteruthius aenobarbus	R	LC
White-bellied Erpornis	Erpornis zantholeuca	R	LC
Campephagidae (Cuckooshrikes)			
Jerdon's Minivet	Pericrocotus albifrons	R*	NT
Fiery Minivet	Pericrocotus igneus	R	NT
Small Minivet	Pericrocotus cinnamomeus	R	LC
Grey-chinned Minivet	Pericrocotus solaris	R	LC
Short-billed Minivet	Pericrocotus brevirostris	R	LC
Long-tailed Minivet	Pericrocotus ethologus	R	LC
Scarlet Minivet	Pericrocotus flammeus	R	LC
Ashy Minivet	Pericrocotus divaricatus	WV	LC
Brown-rumped Minivet	Pericrocotus cantonensis	WV	LC
Rosy Minivet	Pericrocotus roseus	R	LC
Large Cuckooshrike	Coracina javensis	R	LC
Black-winged Cuckooshrike	Lalage melaschistos	R	LC
Black-headed Cuckooshrike	Lalage melanoptera	R	LC
Indochinese Cuckooshrike	Lalage polioptera	R	LC
Lesser Cuckooshrike	Lalage fimbriata	R	LC
Artamidae (Woodswallows & Butcherbirds)			
White-breasted Woodswallow	Artamus leucoryn	R	LC
Ashy Woodswallow	Artamus fuscus	R	LC
Vangidae (Vangas & Allies)			
Bar-winged Flycatcher-shrike	Hemipus picatus	R	LC
Black-winged Flycatcher-shrike	Hemipus hirundinaceus	R	LC
Large Woodshrike	Tephrodornis virgatus	R	LC
Common Woodshrike	Tephrodornis pondicerianus	R	LC
Rufous-winged Philentoma	Philentoma pyrhoptera	R	LC
Maroon-breasted Philentoma	Philentoma velata	R	NT

Common Name	Scientific Name	Seasonal Status	Global Threat
Aegithinidae (Ioras)			
Common Iora	*Aegithina tiphia*	R	LC
Green Iora	*Aegithina viridissima*	R	NT
Great Iora	*Aegithina lafresnayei*	R	LC
Rhipiduridae (Fantails)			
Malaysian Pied Fantail	*Rhipidura javanica*	R	LC
White-browed Fantail	*Rhipidura aureola*	R	LC
White-throated Fantail	*Rhipidura albicollis*	R	LC
Dicruridae (Drongos)			
Black Drongo	*Dicrurus macrocercus*	R	LC
Ashy Drongo	*Dicrurus leucophaeus*	R	LC
Crow-billed Drongo	*Dicrurus annectens*	R	LC
Bronzed Drongo	*Dicrurus aeneus*	R	LC
Lesser Racquet-tailed Drongo	*Dicrurus remifer*	R	LC
Hair-crested Drongo	*Dicrurus hottentottus*	R	LC
Andaman Drongo	*Dicrurus andamanensis*	R	LC
Greater Racquet-tailed Drongo	*Dicrurus paradiseus*	R	LC
Monarchidae (Monarch-flycatchers)			
Black-naped Monarch	*Hypothymis azurea*	R	LC
Indian Paradise-flycatcher	*Terpsiphone paradisi*	R	LC
Amur Paradise-flycatcher	*Terpsiphone incei*	WV	LC
Blyth's Paradise-flycatcher	*Terpsiphone affinis*	R	LC
Platylophidae (Crested Jay)			
Crested Shrike-jay	*Platylophus galericulatus*	R	NT
Laniidae (Shrikes)			
Tiger Shrike	*Lanius tigrinus*	P	LC
Brown Shrike	*Lanius cristatus*	WV	LC
Burmese Shrike	*Lanius collurioides*	R	LC
Bay-backed Shrike	*Lanius vittatus*	V	LC
Long-tailed Shrike	*Lanius schach*	R	LC
Grey-backed Shrike	*Lanius tephronotus*	R	LC
Chinese Grey Shrike	*Lanius sphenocercus*	V	LC
Corvidae (Crows & Jays)			
Malay Black Magpie	*Platysmurus leucopterus*	R	LC
Ratchet-tailed Treepie	*Temnurus temnurus*	R	LC
Racquet-tailed Treepie	*Crypsirina temia*	R	LC
Hooded Treepie	*Crypsirina cucullata*	R*	NT
Rufous Treepie	*Dendrocitta vagabunda*	R	LC
Grey Treepie	*Dendrocitta formosae*	R	LC
Collared Treepie	*Dendrocitta frontalis*	R	LC
Yellow-billed Blue Magpie	*Urocissa flavirostris*	R	LC
Red-billed Blue Magpie	*Urocissa erythroryncha*	R	LC
Common Green Magpie	*Cissa chinensis*	R	LC
Plain-crowned Jay	*Garrulus bispecularis*	R	LC
White-faced Jay	*Garrulus leucotis*	R	LC
Oriental Magpie	*Pica serica*	R	LC
Southern Nutcracker	*Nucifraga hemispila*	R	LC
House Crow	*Corvus splendens*	R	LC
Large-billed Crow	*Corvus macrorhynchos*	R	LC
Stenostiridae (Fairy Flycatcher & Allies)			
Yellow-bellied Fairy-fantail	*Chelidorhynx hypoxanthus*	R	LC
Grey-headed Canary-flycatcher	*Culicicapa ceylonensis*	R	LC
Paridae (Tits & Chickadees)			
Fire-capped Tit	*Cephalopyrus flammiceps*	WV	LC
Yellow-browed Tit	*Sylviparus modestus*	R	LC
Sultan Tit	*Melanochlora sultanea*	R	LC
Coal Tit	*Periparus ater*	R	LC
Rufous-vented Tit	*Periparus rubidiventris*	R	LC
Grey-crested Tit	*Lophophanes dichrous*	R	LC
Black-bibbed Tit	*Poecile hypermelaenus*	R	LC
Green-backed Tit	*Parus monticolus*	R	LC
Cinereous Tit	*Parus cinereus*	R	LC
Japanese Tit	*Parus minor*	R	LC
Yellow-cheeked Tit	*Machlolophus spilonotus*	R	LC

Common Name	Scientific Name	Seasonal Status	Global Threat
Alaudidae (Larks)			
Horsfield's Bushlark	Mirafra javanica	R	LC
Burmese Bushlark	Mirafra microptera	R*	LC
Bengal Bushlark	Mirafra assamica	R	LC
Indochinese Bushlark	Mirafra erythrocephala	R	LC
Asian Short-toed Lark	Alaudala cheleensis	V	LC
Sand Lark	Alaudala raytal	R	LC
Syke's Short-toed Lark	Calandrella dukhunensis	V	LC
Oriental Skylark	Alauda gulgula	R	LC
Cisticolidae (Cisticolas & Allies)			
Zitting Cisticola	Cisticola juncidis	R	LC
Golden-headed Cisticola	Cisticola exilis	R	LC
Striated Prinia	Prinia crinigera	R	LC
Burmese Prinia	Prinia cooki	R	LC
Brown Prinia	Prinia polychroa	R	LC
Rufous-crowned Prinia	Prinia khasiana	R	LC
Hill Prinia	Prinia superciliaris	R	LC
Rufescent Prinia	Prinia rufescens	R	LC
Grey-breasted Prinia	Prinia hodgsonii	R	LC
Yellow-bellied Prinia	Prinia flaviventris	R	LC
Plain Prinia	Prinia inornata	R	LC
Common Tailorbird	Orthotomus sutorius	R	LC
Rufous-tailed Tailorbird	Orthotomus sericeus	R	LC
Dark-necked Tailorbird	Orthotomus atrogularis	R	LC
Ashy Tailorbird	Orthotomus ruficeps	R	LC
Acrocephalidae (Reed-warblers)			
Thick-billed Warbler	Arundinax aedon	WV	LC
Booted Warbler	Iduna caligata	V	LC
Sykes's Warbler	Iduna rama	V	LC
Black-browed Reed-warbler	Acrocephalus bistrigiceps	WV	LC
Large-billed Reed-warbler	Acrocephalus orinus	WV	DD
Blyth's Reed-warbler	Acrocephalus dumetorum	WV	LC
Paddyfield Warbler	Acrocephalus agricola	WV	LC
Blunt-winged Warbler	Acrocephalus concinens	WV	LC
White-browed Reed-warbler	Acrocephalus tangorum	WV	VU
Oriental Reed-warbler	Acrocephalus orientalis	WV	LC
Clamorous Reed-warbler	Acrocephalus stentoreus	R	LC
Pnoepygidae (Cupwings)			
Pygmy Cupwing	Pnoepyga pusilla	R	LC
Scaly-breasted Cupwing	Pnoepyga albiventer	R	LC
Locustellidae (Grasshopper-warblers & Grassbirds)			
Pallas's Grasshopper-warbler	Locustella certhiola	WV	LC
Lanceolated Warbler	Locustella lanceolata	WV	LC
Brown Grasshopper-warbler	Locustella luteoventris	R	LC
Chinese Grasshopper-warbler	Locustella tacsanowskia	WV	LC
Baikal Grasshopper-warbler	Locustella davidi	WV	LC
Spotted Grasshopper-warbler	Locustella thoracica	R	LC
Russet Grasshopper-warbler	Locustella mandelli	R	LC
Striated Grassbird	Megalurus palustris	R	LC
Hirundinidae (Swallows & Martins)			
Eastern House Martin	Delichon lagopodum	WV	LC
Asian House Martin	Delichon dasypus	WV	LC
Nepal House Martin	Delichon nipalense	R	LC
Red-rumped Swallow	Cecropis daurica	R	LC
Rufous-bellied Swallow	Cecropis badia	R	LC
Pacific Swallow	Hirundo tahitica	R	LC
Wire-tailed Swallow	Hirundo smithii	R	LC
Barn Swallow	Hirundo rustica	R	LC
Dusky Crag Martin	Ptyonoprogne concolor	R	LC
Asian Plain Martin	Riparia chinensis	R	LC
Collared Sand Martin	Riparia riparia	WV	LC
Pale Sand Martin	Riparia diluta	WV	LC
Pycnonotidae (Bulbuls)			
Hairy-backed Bulbul	Tricholestes criniger	R	LC
White-throated Bulbul	Alophoixus flaveolus	R	LC

Common Name	Scientific Name	Seasonal Status	Global Threat
Grey-crowned Bulbul	*Alophoixus griseiceps*	R*	LC
Puff-throated Bulbul	*Alophoixus pallidus*	R	LC
Ochraceous Bulbul	*Alophoixus ochraceus*	R	LC
Grey-cheeked Bulbul	*Alophoixus tephrogenys*	R	LC
Yellow-bellied Bulbul	*Alophoixus phaeocephalus*	R	LC
Olive Bulbul	*Iole viridescens*	R	LC
Grey-eyed Bulbul	*Iole propinqua*	R	LC
Buff-vented Bulbul	*Iole charlottae*	R	NT
Ashy Bulbul	*Hemixos flavala*	R	LC
Mountain Bulbul	*Ixos mcclellandii*	R	LC
Streaked Bulbul	*Ixos malaccensis*	R	NT
Black Bulbul	*Hypsipetes leucocephalus*	R	LC
Crested Finchbill	*Spizixos canifrons*	R	LC
Straw-headed Bulbul	*Pycnonotus zeylanicus*	R	CR
Striated Bulbul	*Pycnonotus striatus*	R	LC
Black-crested Bulbul	*Pycnonotus flaviventris*	R	LC
Scaly-breasted Bulbul	*Pycnonotus squamatus*	R	NT
Grey-bellied Bulbul	*Pycnonotus cyaniventris*	R	NT
Red-whiskered Bulbul	*Pycnonotus jocosus*	R	LC
Brown-breasted Bulbul	*Pycnonotus xanthorrhous*	R	LC
Red-vented Bulbul	*Pycnonotus cafer*	R	LC
Sooty-headed Bulbul	*Pycnonotus aurigaster*	R	LC
Pale-eyed Bulbul	*Pycnonotus davisoni*	R*	LC
Stripe-throated Bulbul	*Pycnonotus finlaysoni*	R	LC
Flavescent Bulbul	*Pycnonotus flavescens*	R	LC
Yellow-vented Bulbul	*Pycnonotus goiavier*	R	LC
Olive-winged Bulbul	*Pycnonotus plumosus*	R	LC
Ayeyarwady Bulbul	*Pycnonotus blanfordi*	R	LC
Streak-eared Bulbul	*Pycnonotus conradi*	R	LC
Cream-vented Bulbul	*Pycnonotus simplex*	R	LC
Red-eyed Bulbul	*Pycnonotus brunneus*	R	LC
Spectacled Bulbul	*Pycnonotus erythropthalmos*	R	LC
Puff-backed Bulbul	*Euptilotus eutilotus*	R	NT
Black-headed Bulbul	*Brachypodius atriceps*	R	LC
White-headed Bulbul	*Cerasophila thompsoni*	R	LC
Phylloscopidae (Leaf-warblers)			
Chinese Leaf-warbler	*Phylloscopus yunnanensis*	WV	LC
Yellow-browed Warbler	*Phylloscopus inornatus*	WV	LC
Hume's Leaf-warbler	*Phylloscopus humei*	WV	LC
Lemon-rumped Leaf-warbler	*Phylloscopus chloronotus*	WV	LC
Pallas's Leaf-warbler	*Phylloscopus proregulus*	WV	LC
Sichuan Leaf-warbler	*Phylloscopus forresti*	R	LC
Buff-barred Warbler	*Phylloscopus pulcher*	R	LC
Ashy-throated Warbler	*Phylloscopus maculipennis*	R	LC
Dusky Warbler	*Phylloscopus fuscatus*	WV	LC
Smoky Warbler	*Phylloscopus fuligiventer*	R	LC
Buff-throated Warbler	*Phylloscopus subaffinis*	WV	LC
Tickell's Leaf-warbler	*Phylloscopus affinis*	WV	LC
Yellow-streaked Warbler	*Phylloscopus armandii*	WV	LC
Radde's Warbler	*Phylloscopus schwarzi*	WV	LC
White-spectacled Warbler	*Phylloscopus intermedius*	R	LC
Grey-cheeked Warbler	*Phylloscopus poliogenys*	R	LC
Grey-crowned Warbler	*Phylloscopus tephrocephalus*	R	LC
Martens's Warbler	*Phylloscopus omeiensis*	WV	LC
Alström's Warbler	*Phylloscopus soror*	P	LC
Bianchi's Warbler	*Phylloscopus valentini*	R	LC
Whistler's Warbler	*Phylloscopus whistleri*	R	LC
Eastern Crowned Warbler	*Phylloscopus coronatus*	WV	LC
Chestnut-crowned Warbler	*Phylloscopus castaniceps*	R	LC
Emei Leaf-warbler	*Phylloscopus emeiensis*	WV	LC
Greenish Warbler	*Phylloscopus trochiloides*	WV	LC
Two-barred Warbler	*Phylloscopus plumbeitarsus*	WV	LC
Arctic Warbler	*Phylloscopus borealis*	WV	LC
Pale-legged Leaf-warbler	*Phylloscopus tenellipes*	WV	LC
Sakhalin Leaf-warbler	*Phylloscopus borealoides*	WV	LC

Common Name	Scientific Name	Seasonal Status	Global Threat
Large-billed Leaf-warbler	Phylloscopus magnirostris	R	LC
Yellow-vented Warbler	Phylloscopus cantator	R	LC
Sulphur-breasted Warbler	Phylloscopus ricketti	WV	LC
Claudia's Leaf-warbler	Phylloscopus claudiae	WV	LC
Blyth's Leaf-warbler	Phylloscopus reguloides	R	LC
Grey-hooded Warbler	Phylloscopus xanthoschistos	R	LC
White-tailed Leaf-warbler	Phylloscopus intensior	R	LC
Kloss's Leaf-warbler	Phylloscopus ogilviegranti	WV	LC
Scotocercidae (Bush-warblers)			
Slaty-bellied Tesia	Tesia olivea	R	LC
Grey-bellied Tesia	Tesia cyaniventer	R	LC
Chestnut-crowned Bush-warbler	Cettia major	R	LC
Grey-sided Bush-warbler	Cettia brunnifrons	R	LC
Chestnut-headed Tesia	Cettia castaneocoronata	R	LC
Pale-footed Bush-warbler	Hemitesia pallidipes	R	LC
Asian Stubtail	Urosphena squameiceps	WV	LC
Yellow-bellied Warbler	Abroscopus superciliaris	R	LC
Rufous-faced Warbler	Abroscopus albogularis	R	LC
Black-faced Warbler	Abroscopus schisticeps	R	LC
Mountain Tailorbird	Phyllergates cucullatus	R	LC
Broad-billed Warbler	Tickellia hodgsoni	R	LC
Brownish-flanked Bush-warbler	Horornis fortipes	R	LC
Hume's Bush warbler	Horornis brunnescens	R	LC
Aberrant Bush-warbler	Horornis flavolivaceus	R	LC
Manchurian Bush-warbler	Horornis canturians	WV	LC
Aegithalidae (Long-tailed Tits)			
Black-throated Tit	Aegithalos concinnus	R	LC
Black-browed Tit	Aegithalos bonvaloti	R	LC
Burmese Tit	Aegithalos sharpei	R*	LC
Sylviidae (Old World Warblers & Parrotbills)			
Fire-tailed Myzornis	Myzornis pyrrhoura	R	LC
Golden-breasted Fulvetta	Lioparus chrysotis	R	LC
Yellow-eyed Babbler	Chrysomma sinense	R	LC
Jerdon's Babbler	Chrysomma altirostre	R	VU
White-browed Fulvetta	Fulvetta vinipectus	R	LC
Brown-throated Fulvetta	Fulvetta ludlowi	R	LC
Manipur Fulvetta	Fulvetta manipurensis	R	LC
Spot-breasted Parrotbill	Paradoxornis guttaticollis	R	LC
Rufous-headed Parrotbill	Psittiparus bakeri	R	LC
Grey-headed Parrotbill	Psittiparus gularis	R	LC
Great Parrotbill	Conostoma aemodium	R	LC
Brown Parrotbill	Cholornis unicolor	R	LC
Short-tailed Parrotbill	Neosuthora davidiana	R	LC
Fulvous Parrotbill	Suthora fulvifrons	R	LC
Black-throated Parrotbill	Suthora nipalensis	R	LC
Golden Parrotbill	Suthora verreauxi	R	LC
Pale-billed Parrotbill	Chleuasicus atrosuperciliaris	R	LC
Brown-winged Parrotbill	Sinosuthora brunnea	R	LC
Zosteropidae (White-eyes & Yuhinas)			
White-collared Yuhina	Yuhina diademata	R	LC
Striated Yuhina	Yuhina castaniceps	R	LC
Black-chinned Yuhina	Yuhina nigrimenta	R	LC
Stripe-throated Yuhina	Yuhina gularis	R	LC
Whiskered Yuhina	Yuhina flavicollis	R	LC
Burmese Yuhina	Yuhina humilis	R	LC
Rufous-vented Yuhina	Yuhina occipitalis	R	LC
White-naped Yuhina	Yuhina bakeri	R	LC
Chestnut-flanked White-eye	Zosterops erythropleurus	R	LC
Indian White-eye	Zosterops palpebrosus	R	LC
Hume's White-eye	Zosterops auriventer	R	LC
Swinhoe's White-eye	Zosterops japonicus	R	LC
Timaliidae (Scimitar-babblers & Allies)			
Bar-winged Wren-babbler	Spelaeornis troglodytoides	R	LC
Chin Hills Wren-babbler	Spelaeornis oatesi	R	LC
Grey-bellied Wren-babbler	Spelaeornis reptatus	R	LC

Common Name	Scientific Name	Seasonal Status	Global Threat
Red-billed Scimitar-babbler	*Pomatorhinus ochraceiceps*	R	LC
Brown-crowned Scimitar-babbler	*Pomatorhinus phayrei*	R	LC
Slender-billed Scimitar-babbler	*Pomatorhinus superciliaris*	R	LC
White-browed Scimitar-babbler	*Pomatorhinus schisticeps*	R	LC
Streak-breasted Scimitar-babbler	*Pomatorhinus ruficollis*	R	LC
Large Scimitar-babbler	*Erythrogenys hypoleucos*	R	LC
Rusty-cheeked Scimitar-babbler	*Erythrogenys erythrogenys*	R	LC
Spot-breasted Scimitar-babbler	*Erythrogenys mcclellandi*	R	LC
Black-streaked Scimitar-babbler	*Erythrogenys gravivox*	R	LC
Grey-throated Babbler	*Stachyris nigriceps*	R	LC
Chevron-breasted Babbler	*Stachyris roberti*	R	NT
Spot-necked Babbler	*Stachyris strialata*	R	LC
Snowy-throated Babbler	*Stachyris oglei*	R	VU
Chestnut-capped Babbler	*Timalia pileata*	R	LC
Pin-striped Tit-babbler	*Mixornis gularis*	R	LC
Golden Babbler	*Cyanoderma chrysaeum*	R	LC
Chestnut-winged Babbler	*Cyanoderma erythropterum*	R	LC
Rufous-capped Babbler	*Cyanoderma ruficeps*	R	LC
Buff-chested Babbler	*Cyanoderma ambiguum*	R	LC
Rufous-fronted Babbler	*Cyanoderma rufifrons*	R	LC
Pellorneidae (Ground Babblers)			
Rufous-crowned Babbler	*Malacopteron magnum*	R	NT
Moustached Babbler	*Malacopteron magnirostre*	R	LC
White-hooded Babbler	*Gampsorhynchus rufulus*	R	LC
Collared Babbler	*Gampsorhynchus torquatus*	R	LC
Rusty-capped Fulvetta	*Schoeniparus dubius*	R	LC
Rufous-throated Fulvetta	*Schoeniparus rufogularis*	R	LC
Yellow-throated Fulvetta	*Schoeniparus cinereus*	R	LC
Rufous-winged Fulvetta	*Schoeniparus castaneceps*	R	LC
Puff-throated Babbler	*Pellorneum ruficeps*	R	LC
Black-capped Babbler	*Pellorneum nigrocapitatum*	R	LC
Spot-throated Babbler	*Pellorneum albiventre*	R	LC
Short-tailed Babbler	*Trichastoma malaccense*	R	NT
Ferruginous Babbler	*Trichastoma bicolor*	R	LC
White-chested Babbler	*Trichastoma rostratum*	R	NT
Buff-breasted Babbler	*Trichastoma tickelli*	R	LC
Abbott's Babbler	*Malacocincla abbotti*	R	LC
Variable Limestone Babbler	*Gypsophila crispifrons*	R	LC
Streaked Wren-babbler	*Turdinus brevicaudatus*	R	LC
Eyebrowed Wren-babbler	*Napothera epilepidota*	R	LC
Naung Mung Wren-babbler	*Rimator naungmungensis*	R	VU
Long-billed Wren-babbler	*Rimator malacoptilus*	R	LC
Chinese Grass-babbler	*Graminicola striatus*	R	VU
Leiotrichidae (Laughingthrushes & Allies)			
Brown-cheeked Fulvetta	*Alcippe poioicephala*	R	LC
Nepal Fulvetta	*Alcippe nipalensis*	R	LC
Grey-cheeked Fulvetta	*Alcippe morrisonia*	R	LC
Striated Laughingthrush	*Grammatoptila striata*	R	LC
Himalayan Cutia	*Cutia nipalensis*	R	LC
Striated Babbler	*Turdoides earlei*	R	LC
Slender-billed Babbler	*Turdoides longirostris*	H	VU
White-throated Babbler	*Turdoides gularis*	R*	LC
Chinese Hwamei	*Garrulax canorus*	V	LC
Spot-breasted Laughingthrush	*Garrulax merulinus*	R	LC
Lesser Necklaced Laughingthrush	*Garrulax monileger*	R	LC
White-crested Laughingthrush	*Garrulax leucolophus*	R	LC
Spotted Laughingthrush	*Garrulax ocellatus*	R	LC
White-necked Laughingthrush	*Garrulax strepitans*	R	LC
Western Moustached Laughingthrush	*Garrulax cineraceus*	R	LC
Rufous-chinned Laughingthrush	*Garrulax rufogularis*	R	LC
White-browed Laughingthrush	*Garrulax sannio*	R	LC
Chestnut-backed Laughingthrush	*Garrulax nuchalis*	R	NT
Black-throated Laughingthrush	*Garrulax chinensis*	R	LC
Greater Necklaced Laughingthrush	*Garrulax pectoralis*	R	LC
Mount Victoria Babax	*Garrulax woodi*	R	LC

Common Name	Scientific Name	Seasonal Status	Global Threat
Chinese Babax	Garrulax lanceolatus	R	LC
White-throated Laughingthrush	Garrulax albogularis	R	LC
Grey-sided Laughingthrush	Garrulax caerulatus	R	LC
Rufous-necked Laughingthrush	Garrulax ruficollis	R	LC
Yellow-throated Laughingthrush	Garrulax galbanus	R	LC
Rufous-vented Laughingthrush	Garrulax gularis	R	LC
Scaly Laughingthrush	Trochalopteron subunicolor	R	LC
Brown-capped Laughingthrush	Trochalopteron austeni	R	LC
Blue-winged Laughingthrush	Trochalopteron squamatum	R	LC
Striped Laughingthrush	Trochalopteron virgatum	R	LC
Black-faced Laughingthrush	Trochalopteron affine	R	LC
Red-tailed Laughingthrush	Trochalopteron milnei	R	LC
Assam Laughingthrush	Trochalopteron chrysopterum	R	LC
Silver-eared Laughingthrush	Trochalopteron melanostigma	R	LC
Long-tailed Sibia	Heterophasia picaoides	R	LC
Beautiful Sibia	Heterophasia pulchella	R	LC
Dark-backed Sibia	Heterophasia melanoleuca	R	LC
Black-headed Sibia	Heterophasia desgodinsi	R	LC
Grey Sibia	Heterophasia gracilis	R	LC
Silver-eared Mesia	Leiothrix argentauris	R	LC
Red-billed Leiothrix	Leiothrix lutea	R	LC
Rufous-backed Sibia	Leioptila annectens	R	LC
Red-tailed Minla	Minla ignotincta	R	LC
Red-faced Liocichla	Liocichla phoenicea	R	LC
Scarlet-faced Liocichla	Liocichla ripponi	R	LC
Streak-throated Barwing	Actinodura waldeni	R	LC
Rusty-fronted Barwing	Actinodura egertoni	R	LC
Western Spectacled Barwing	Actinodura ramsayi	R	LC
Eastern Spectacled Barwing	Actinodura radcliffei	R	LC
Blue-winged Minla	Siva cyanouroptera	R	LC
Bar-throated Minla	Chrysominla strigula	R	LC
Certhiidae (Treecreepers)			
Rusty-flanked Treecreeper	Certhia nipalensis	R	LC
Manipur Treecreeper	Certhia manipurensis	R	LC
Bar-tailed Treecreeper	Certhia himalayana	R	LC
Hodgson's Treecreeper	Certhia hodgsoni	R	LC
Sittidae (Nuthatches)			
Chestnut-vented Nuthatch	Sitta nagaensis	R	LC
Chestnut-bellied Nuthatch	Sitta cinnamoventris	R	LC
Burmese Nuthatch	Sitta neglecta	R	LC
White-tailed Nuthatch	Sitta himalayensis	R	LC
White-browed Nuthatch	Sitta victoriae	R*	EN
Velvet-fronted Nuthatch	Sitta frontalis	R	LC
Giant Nuthatch	Sitta magna	R	EN
Beautiful Nuthatch	Sitta formosa	R	VU
Wallcreeper	Tichodroma muraria	WV	LC
Troglodytidae (Wrens)			
Northern Wren	Troglodytes troglodytes	R	LC
Cinclidae (Dippers)			
White-throated Dipper	Cinclus cinclus	R	LC
Brown Dipper	Cinclus pallasii	R	LC
Sturnidae (Starlings)			
Common Starling	Sturnus vulgaris	WV	LC
Rosy Starling	Pastor roseus	WV	LC
Purple-backed Starling	Agropsar sturninus	P	LC
Asian Pied Starling	Gracupica contra	R	LC
Black-collared Starling	Gracupica nigricollis	R	LC
Brahminy Starling	Sturnia pagodarum	WV	LC
White-shouldered Starling	Sturnia sinensis	WV	LC
Chestnut-tailed Starling	Sturnia malabarica	R	LC
White-cheeked Starling	Spodiopsar cineraceus	WV	LC
Common Myna	Acridotheres tristis	R	LC
Burmese Myna	Acridotheres burmannicus	R	LC
Jungle Myna	Acridotheres fuscus	R	LC
Collared Myna	Acridotheres albocinctus	R	LC

Common Name	Scientific Name	Seasonal Status	Global Threat
Great Myna	Acridotheres grandis	R	LC
Crested Myna	Acridotheres cristatellus	R	LC
Spot-winged Starling	Saroglossa spilopterus	WV	LC
Common Hill Myna	Gracula religiosa	R	LC
Golden-crested Myna	Ampeliceps coronatus	R	LC
Asian Glossy Starling	Aplonis panayensis	R	LC
Turdidae (Thrushes)			
Grandala	Grandala coelicolor	R	LC
Long-tailed Thrush	Zoothera dixoni	R	LC
Alpine Thrush	Zoothera mollissima	R	LC
Himalayan Thrush	Zoothera salimalii	R	LC
Dark-sided Thrush	Zoothera marginata	R	LC
Long-billed Thrush	Zoothera monticola	R	LC
White's Thrush	Zoothera aurea	WV	LC
Scaly Thrush	Zoothera dauma	R	LC
Purple Cochoa	Cochoa purpurea	R	LC
Green Cochoa	Cochoa viridis	R	LC
Siberian Thrush	Geokichla sibirica	P	LC
Orange-headed Thrush	Geokichla citrina	R	LC
Song Thrush	Turdus philomelos	V	LC
Chinese Blackbird	Turdus mandarinus	WV	LC
Grey-winged Blackbird	Turdus boulboul	R	LC
Japanese Thrush	Turdus cardis	WV	LC
Black-breasted Thrush	Turdus dissimilis	R	LC
Tickell's Thrush	Turdus unicolor	V	LC
Eyebrowed Thrush	Turdus obscurus	WV	LC
Grey-sided Thrush	Turdus feae	WV	VU
White-collared Blackbird	Turdus albocinctus	WV	LC
Chestnut Thrush	Turdus rubrocanus	WV	LC
Naumann's Thrush	Turdus naumanni	WV	LC
Dusky Thrush	Turdus eunomus	WV	LC
Black-throated Thrush	Turdus atrogularis	WV	LC
Rufous-throated Thrush	Turdus ruficollis	WV	LC
Muscicapidae (Old World Flycatchers & Chats)			
Oriental Magpie-robin	Copsychus saularis	R	LC
White-rumped Shama	Kittacincla malabarica	R	LC
Dark-sided Flycatcher	Muscicapa sibirica	R	LC
Ferruginous Flycatcher	Muscicapa ferruginea	R	LC
Brown-breasted Flycatcher	Muscicapa muttui	BV	LC
Brown-streaked Flycatcher	Muscicapa williamsoni	R	LC
Asian Brown Flycatcher	Muscicapa dauurica	R	LC
Rufous-bellied Niltava	Niltava sundara	R	LC
Small Niltava	Niltava macgrigoriae	R	LC
Large Vivid Niltava	Niltava oatesi	WV	LC
Large Niltava	Niltava grandis	R	LC
Blue-and-white Flycatcher	Cyanoptila cyanomelana	P	LC
Verditer Flycatcher	Eumyias thalassinus	R	LC
White-gorgeted Flycatcher	Anthipes monileger	R	LC
Rufous-browed Flycatcher	Anthipes solitaris	R	LC
Fulvous-chested Jungle-flycatcher	Cyornis olivaceus	R	LC
Pale Blue-flycatcher	Cyornis unicolor	R	LC
Pale-chinned Flycatcher	Cyornis poliogenys	R	LC
Large Blue-flycatcher	Cyornis magnirostris	R	LC
Hill Blue-flycatcher	Cyornis banyumas	R	LC
Indochinese Blue-flycatcher	Cyornis sumatrensis	R	LC
Chinese Blue-flycatcher	Cyornis glaucicomans	WV	LC
Hainan Blue-flycatcher	Cyornis hainanus	R	LC
Blue-throated Blue-flycatcher	Cyornis rubeculoides	R	LC
White-tailed Flycatcher	Cyornis concretus	R	LC
Gould's Shortwing	Heteroxenicus stellatus	R	LC
Rusty-bellied Shortwing	Brachypteryx hyperythra	R	NT
Lesser Shortwing	Brachypteryx leucophris	R	LC
Himalayan Shortwing	Brachypteryx cruralis	R	LC
Indian Blue Robin	Larvivora brunnea	R	LC
Siberian Blue Robin	Larvivora cyane	WV	LC

Common Name	Scientific Name	Seasonal Status	Global Threat
White-bellied Redstart	Hodgsonius phaenicuroides	R	LC
Bluethroat	Cyanecula svecica	WV	LC
Firethroat	Calliope pectardens	WV	NT
Siberian Rubythroat	Calliope calliope	WV	LC
Chinese Rubythroat	Calliope tschebaiewi	R	LC
White-tailed Blue Robin	Myiomela leucura	R	LC
Rufous-breasted Bush-robin	Tarsiger hyperythrus	R	LC
Orange-flanked Bush-robin	Tarsiger cyanurus	WV	LC
Himalayan Bush-robin	Tarsiger rufilatus	R	LC
White-browed Bush-robin	Tarsiger indicus	R	LC
Golden Bush-robin	Tarsiger chrysaeus	R	LC
Little Forktail	Enicurus scouleri	R	LC
Slaty-backed Forktail	Enicurus schistaceus	R	LC
Chestnut-naped Forktail	Enicurus ruficapillus	R	NT
Black-backed Forktail	Enicurus immaculatus	R	LC
White-crowned Forktail	Enicurus leschenaulti	R	LC
Spotted Forktail	Enicurus maculatus	R	LC
Blue-fronted Robin	Cinclidium frontale	R	LC
Blue Whistling-thrush	Myophonus caeruleus	R	LC
Green-backed Flycatcher	Ficedula elisae	P	LC
Yellow-rumped Flycatcher	Ficedula zanthopygia	P	LC
Mugimaki Flycatcher	Ficedula mugimaki	P	LC
Narcissus Flycatcher	Ficedula narcissina	P	LC
Slaty-backed Flycatcher	Ficedula erithacus	R	LC
Slaty-blue Flycatcher	Ficedula tricolor	R	LC
Snowy-browed Flycatcher	Ficedula hyperythra	R	LC
Pygmy Blue-flycatcher	Ficedula hodgsoni	R	LC
Rufous-gorgeted Flycatcher	Ficedula strophiata	R	LC
Sapphire Flycatcher	Ficedula sapphira	R	LC
Ultramarine Flycatcher	Ficedula superciliaris	R	LC
Little Pied Flycatcher	Ficedula westermanni	R	LC
Red-breasted Flycatcher	Ficedula parva	V	LC
Taiga Flycatcher	Ficedula albicilla	WV	LC
Blue-fronted Redstart	Phoenicurus frontalis	R	LC
White-throated Redstart	Phoenicurus schisticeps	R	LC
White-capped Water-redstart	Phoenicurus leucocephalus	R	LC
Plumbeous Water-redstart	Phoenicurus fuliginosus	R	LC
Black Redstart	Phoenicurus ochruros	R	LC
Daurian Redstart	Phoenicurus auroreus	WV	LC
Hodgson's Redstart	Phoenicurus hodgsoni	WV	LC
Blue-capped Rock-thrush	Monticola cinclorhyncha	V	LC
Chestnut-bellied Rock-thrush	Monticola rufiventris	R	LC
White-throated Rock-thrush	Monticola gularis	WV	LC
Blue Rock-thrush	Monticola solitarius	WV	LC
Jerdon's Bushchat	Saxicola jerdoni	R	LC
Grey Bushchat	Saxicola ferreus	R	LC
Pied Bushchat	Saxicola caprata	R	LC
White-tailed Stonechat	Saxicola leucurus	R	LC
Siberian Stonechat	Saxicola maurus	R	LC
Amur Stonechat	Saxicola stejnegeri	WV	LC
Isabelline Wheatear	Oenanthe isabellina	V	LC
Regulidae (Kinglets & Firecrests)			
Goldcrest	Regulus regulus	R	LC
Elachuridae (Elachura)			
Spotted Elachura	Elachura formosa	R	LC
Irenidae (Fairy-bluebirds)			
Asian Fairy-bluebird	Irena puella	R	LC
Chloropseidae (Leafbirds)			
Greater Green Leafbird	Chloropsis sonnerati	R	VU
Lesser Green Leafbird	Chloropsis cyanopogon	R	NT
Golden-fronted Leafbird	Chloropsis aurifrons	R	LC
Orange-bellied Leafbird	Chloropsis hardwickii	R	LC
Blue-winged Leafbird	Chloropsis moluccensis	R	LC
Dicaeidae (Flowerpeckers)			
Yellow-breasted Flowerpecker	Prionochilus maculatus	R	LC

Common Name	Scientific Name	Seasonal Status	Global Threat
Crimson-breasted Flowerpecker	Prionochilus percussus	R	LC
Yellow-bellied Flowerpecker	Dicaeum melanozanthum	R	LC
Yellow-vented Flowerpecker	Dicaeum chrysorrheum	R	LC
Thick-billed Flowerpecker	Dicaeum agile	R	LC
Orange-bellied Flowerpecker	Dicaeum trigonostigma	R	LC
Pale-billed Flowerpecker	Dicaeum erythrorhynchos	R	LC
Plain Flowerpecker	Dicaeum minullum	R	LC
Scarlet-backed Flowerpecker	Dicaeum cruentatum	R	LC
Fire-breasted Flowerpecker	Dicaeum ignipectus	R	LC
Nectariniidae (Sunbirds)			
Long-billed Spiderhunter	Arachnothera robusta	R	LC
Little Spiderhunter	Arachnothera longirostra	R	LC
Purple-naped Spiderhunter	Arachnothera hypogrammica	R	LC
Yellow-eared Spiderhunter	Arachnothera chrysogenys	R	LC
Streaked Spiderhunter	Arachnothera magna	R	LC
Spectacled Spiderhunter	Arachnothera flavigaster	R	LC
Grey-breasted Spiderhunter	Arachnothera modesta	R	LC
Ruby-cheeked Sunbird	Chalcoparia singalensis	R	LC
Plain Sunbird	Anthreptes simplex	R	LC
Brown-throated Sunbird	Anthreptes malacensis	R	LC
Red-throated Sunbird	Anthreptes rhodolaemus	R	NT
Purple-rumped Sunbird	Leptocoma zeylonica	V	LC
Maroon-bellied Sunbird	Leptocoma brasiliana	R	LC
Copper-throated Sunbird	Leptocoma calcostetha	R	LC
Purple Sunbird	Cinnyris asiaticus	R	LC
Olive-backed Sunbird	Cinnyris jugularis	R	LC
Fire-tailed Sunbird	Aethopyga ignicauda	R	LC
Black-throated Sunbird	Aethopyga saturata	R	LC
Green-tailed Sunbird	Aethopyga nipalensis	R	LC
Gould's Sunbird	Aethopyga gouldiae	R	LC
Crimson Sunbird	Aethopyga siparaja	R	LC
Prunellidae (Accentors)			
Alpine Accentor	Prunella collaris	R	LC
Maroon-backed Accentor	Prunella immaculata	R	LC
Rufous-breasted Accentor	Prunella strophiata	R	LC
Ploceidae (Weavers)			
Asian Golden Weaver	Ploceus hypoxanthus	R	NT
Streaked Weaver	Ploceus manyar	R	LC
Baya Weaver	Ploceus philippinus	R	LC
Black-breasted Weaver	Ploceus benghalensis	H	LC
Estrildidae (Waxbills)			
Red Avadavat	Amandava amandava	R	LC
Indian Silverbill	Euodice malabarica	R	LC
Java Sparrow	Padda oryzivora	I	EN
White-rumped Munia	Lonchura striata	R	LC
Scaly-breasted Munia	Lonchura punctulata	R	LC
White-bellied Munia	Lonchura leucogastra	R	LC
Chestnut Munia	Lonchura atricapilla	R	LC
Pin-tailed Parrotfinch	Erythrura prasina	R	LC
Passeridae (Old World Sparrows)			
House Sparrow	Passer domesticus	R	LC
Russet Sparrow	Passer cinnamomeus	R	LC
Plain-backed Sparrow	Passer flaveolus	R	LC
Eurasian Tree Sparrow	Passer montanus	R	LC
Motacillidae (Pipits & Wagtails)			
Forest Wagtail	Dendronanthus indicus	WV	LC
Tree Pipit	Anthus trivialis	V	LC
Olive-backed Pipit	Anthus hodgsoni	R	LC
Red-throated Pipit	Anthus cervinus	WV	LC
Rosy Pipit	Anthus roseatus	R	LC
Buff-bellied Pipit	Anthus rubescens	WV	LC
Water Pipit	Anthus spinoletta	WV	LC
Upland Pipit	Anthus sylvanus	R	LC
Richard's Pipit	Anthus richardi	WV	LC
Paddyfield Pipit	Anthus rufulus	R	LC

Common Name	Scientific Name	Seasonal Status	Global Threat
Blyth's Pipit	*Anthus godlewskii*	WV	LC
Long-billed Pipit	*Anthus similis*	R	LC
Grey Wagtail	*Motacilla cinerea*	WV	LC
Citrine Wagtail	*Motacilla citreola*	WV	LC
Western Yellow Wagtail	*Motacilla flava*	V	LC
Eastern Yellow Wagtail	*Motacilla tschutschensis*	WV	LC
White Wagtail	*Motacilla alba*	R	LC
Fringillidae (Finches)			
Brambling	*Fringilla montifringilla*	WV	LC
Collared Grosbeak	*Mycerobas affinis*	R	LC
Spot-winged Grosbeak	*Mycerobas melanozanthos*	R	LC
White-winged Grosbeak	*Mycerobas carnipes*	R	LC
Chinese Grosbeak	*Eophona migratoria*	WV	LC
Common Rosefinch	*Carpodacus erythrinus*	R	LC
Scarlet Finch	*Carpodacus sipahi*	R	LC
Dark-rumped Rosefinch	*Carpodacus edwardsii*	R	LC
Sharpe's Rosefinch	*Carpodacus verreauxii*	R	LC
Vinaceous Rosefinch	*Carpodacus vinaceus*	R	LC
Long-tailed Rosefinch	*Carpodacus sibiricus*	V	LC
Red-fronted Rosefinch	*Carpodacus puniceus*	R	LC
Crimson-browed Finch	*Carpodacus subhimachalus*	R	LC
Chinese White-browed Rosefinch	*Carpodacus dubius*	R	LC
Brown Bullfinch	*Pyrrhula nipalensis*	R	LC
Grey-headed Bullfinch	*Pyrrhula erythaca*	R	LC
Blanford's Rosefinch	*Agraphospiza rubescens*	R	LC
Gold-naped Finch	*Pyrrhoplectes epauletta*	R	LC
Dark-breasted Rosefinch	*Procarduelis nipalensis*	R	LC
Plain Mountain-finch	*Leucosticte nemoricola*	R	LC
Brandt's Mountain-finch	*Leucosticte brandti*	R	LC
Yellow-breasted Greenfinch	*Chloris spinoides*	R	LC
Black-headed Greenfinch	*Chloris ambigua*	R	LC
Red Crossbill	*Loxia curvirostra*	R	LC
Tibetan Siskin	*Spinus thibetanus*	R	LC
Emberizidae (Old World Buntings)			
Crested Bunting	*Emberiza lathami*	R	LC
Black-headed Bunting	*Emberiza melanocephala*	WV	LC
Red-headed Bunting	*Emberiza bruniceps*	V	LC
Chestnut-eared Bunting	*Emberiza fucata*	WV	LC
Godlewski's Bunting	*Emberiza godlewskii*	R	LC
Yellow-throated Bunting	*Emberiza elegans*	WV	LC
Pallas's Bunting	*Emberiza pallasi*	WV	LC
Yellow-breasted Bunting	*Emberiza aureola*	WV	CR
Little Bunting	*Emberiza pusilla*	WV	LC
Black-faced Bunting	*Emberiza spodocephala*	WV	LC
Chestnut Bunting	*Emberiza rutila*	WV	LC
Tristram's Bunting	*Emberiza tristrami*	WV	LC

FURTHER READING

King, B. F., Dickinson, E. C. & Woodcock, M. W. 1975. *A Field Guide to the Birds of South-East Asia*. Collins. London.

Kyaw Nyunt Lwin & Khin Ma Ma Thwin. 2005. *Birds of Myanmar*. Silkworm. Chiang Mai.

Rasmussen, P. C. & Anderton, J. C. 2012. *Birds of South Asia*. The Ripley Guide. Vols 1 & 2 (2nd edn). National Museum of Natural History – Smithsonian Institution. Michigan State. University and Lynx Edicions, Washington, DC, Michigan and Barcelona.

Robson, C. R. 2008. *A Field Guide to the Birds of South-East Asia*. New Holland Publishers. London.

Smythies, B. E. 1986. *The Birds of Burma* (3rd edn). Nimrod Press. Liss, UK.

Wells, D. R. 1999. *The Birds of the Thai-Malay Peninsula*, Vol. 1. Non-Passerines. Academic Press. London.

Wells, D. R. 1999. *The Birds of the Thai-Malay Peninsula*, Vol. 2. Passerines. A & C Black. London.

Yong, D. L. & Low, B. W. 2018. *The 125 Best Birdwatching Sites in Southeast Asia*. John Beaufoy Publishing. Oxford.

LOCAL CONSERVATION ORGANIZATIONS

Myanmar Bird and Nature Society (MBNS) First non-profit organization dedicated to research into and protection of birds and nature in Myanmar. More than 600 members. www.myanmarbirdnaturesociety.com

Biodiversity and Nature Conservation Association (BANCA) Birdlife partner in Myanmar with programmes working on Baer's Pochard, Spoon-billed Sandpiper, Helmeted Hornbill, Gurney's Pitta and Yellow-breasted Bunting. www.banca-env.org

Friends of Wildlife (FOW) Effective local NGO working on range of conservation issues for Myanmar's unique ecosystems, including birds. www.fowmyanmar.org

KEY INTERNATIONAL NGOS WORKING IN MYANMAR

Fauna and Flora International (FFI) www.fauna-flora.org/countries/myanmar

International Union for Conservation of Nature (IUCN) www.iucn.org/regions/asia/countries/myanmar

The Nature Conservancy www.nature.org/en-us/about-us/where-we-work/asia-pacific/myanmar/

Smithsonian Institution global.si.edu/countries/myanmar

Wildlife Conservation Society (WCS) myanmar.wcs.org

World Wide Fund for Nature (WWF) www.wwf.org.mm

ACKNOWLEDGEMENTS

This book is dedicated to our fellow Burmese birders and photographers especially Thet Win, Lay Win, Nyan Lin and Branshaung who join us in the field, have led many of the ornithological explorations across the country and are continuing to document birds in Myanmar's furthest corners.

We also thank the men and women of the Ministry of Natural Resources and Environmental Conservation for their tireless commitment to conserving the magnificent avifauna of Myanmar. In particular we thank His Excellency U Ohn Winn, Minister of MOECAF, Dr Nyi Nyi Kyaw, Director General of the Forest Department, and Dr Naing Zaw Htun, Director, Nature and Wildlife Conservation Division, for their continued support for research and conservation of Myanmar's birds.

Our explorations across the country were not possible without our conservation colleagues from the Wildlife Conservation Society, including U Than Myint, U Saw Htun, U Than Zaw, U Naing Lin and Kyaw Zay Ya as well as many more.

We thank our fellow birders for their support and encouragement concerning the birds of Myanmar and surrounding areas: Colin Poole, William Duckworth, James Eaton, Rob Hutchinson, Frank Rheindt, Phil Round, Simon Mahood and Craig Robson continue to challenge and inspire.